W9-AAC-706

The Telluride Cookbook

Recipes From
Telluride's Best Restaurants
& Caterers

3D PRESS

The Creative Dimensions of
Writing, Photography and Design

3D PRESS
P.O. Box 884
Telluride, CO 81435

Copyright © 1995 by 3D PRESS
Cover Illustration by Roger Mason
Photography by Doug Berry / Telluride Stock Photography

No part of this book may be reproduced
in any form or by any means
without permission from the publisher.

Text by Michelle Kodis
Compiled and Edited by Dave Rich
Designed by Daiva Chesonis / Vision Design

ISBN 0-9634607-6-5

PRINTED IN THE U.S.A.
by
Pyramid Printing
1119 North 1st Street
Grand Junction, CO 80501

"If this ain't paradise, heaven can wait."

-Dizzy Gillespie

ACKNOWLEDGMENTS

I would like to thank the following people without whose help this book would not have been possible: Myra Rich for her editing, for writing the back cover text and for her many grueling hours spent in the test kitchen; Daiva Chesonis / Vision Design for her graphic design work; Annie Kuhles for her invaluable help in collecting recipes and organizing interviews; Sarah Rich for her time testing recipes; Roger Mason for his wonderful painting which graces the front cover; Doug Berry / Telluride Stock Photography for the many fantastic photographs adorning the interior; Between the Covers Bookstore and Bookworks for their design input and patience in answering my many questions; the time and creativity of all the chefs and restaurant owners who contributed; Marc Terrien / Pyramid Printing of Grand Junction, Colorado for his help in pre-press decisions and for printing this book; and, last but certainly not least, Michelle Kodis whose writing skills and diligent research made this book a reality.

-*Dave Rich, publisher*

CONTENTS

TELLURIDE HISTORY

Founded in 1878, Telluride has a history as colorful as the autumnal gold of the fall aspens. Originally christened Columbia, the fledgling town was forced to change its name in 1887 because of post office confusion with another mining camp named Columbia, this one in California. Thus, Telluride, named for the ore of the nonmetallic element tellurium that is found in combination with gold and silver, began its ascent to the summit of the mining industry. The young town was full of promise. Lots were $1 in 1881 and houses sprang up, ranging in size and scope from the simple wooden shacks of the miners to the grand Victorian mansions of the mine owners.

The allure of money and success drifted through Telluride in a palpable wave of greed and desire. The area seemed geographically poised at exactly the right spot: on the southwestern end of the Colorado Mineral Belt, a hearty strip of crustal deformation containing fissures packed with gold, silver, lead and zinc ore. Indeed, the mines scattered high above the Telluride valley churned out millions of dollars in precious metals. Prospectors felt themselves pulled toward Telluride as if by some invisible, Herculean magnet.

The pace of Telluride reached a near frenzy by the close of the century. At the apex of the gold rush, nearly 5,000 people inhabited the "Town Without A Bellyache." The famous Tomboy Mine was one of the world's greatest gold producers. Prostitutes worked out of rundown houses called cribs on Pacific Street, selling their bodily wares to the work-weary and lonely. There were dances, plays, marching bands and thousands of minds intent on a single communal goal: money. Inevitably, lawlessness was commonplace. Butch Cassidy pulled one of his first heists in Telluride, robbing the San Miguel Valley Bank in 1889 and lending the town an image of wild notoriety.

Despite the patina of success, a vein of discontent began to pulse underneath the bright festivities of Main Street life. Workers at the profitable Smuggler-Union mine, bitter over low wages and back-breaking work, went on strike. Years of conflict between management and labor followed, pulling Telluride into a gradual decline. The final blow came when the area's mines shut down in 1953. Many left town, and those who stayed sensed that the potent energy that had marked the area's heyday had begun to slip through their fingers like sand on a beach. For over 20 years,

Telluride was an official Colorado ghost town. The million dollar homes of today sold for back taxes and the population dropped into the hundreds. Then the town had its second rush, discovering a mother lode of another sort: white gold.

Snow. It flies in sheets of white rage across the mountain mesas, collecting in pockets of hard-packed drift and clinging to the exposed trunks of stripped down trees. It traps cars, grounds planes, transforms roads into ribbons of ice and falls in glorious overabundance onto the tops of the mountains. It also put Telluride back on the map.

Skiing was popular in Telluride as far back as the 1930s, when the Ski-Hi Ski Club pulled members up a small run on an unsteady rope tow. Nearly 40 years later, a wealthy entrepreneur from Beverly Hills, Joe Zoline, happened upon Telluride, finding here an opportunity "to do something beautiful and constructive." His determined vision for a ski area in Telluride resulted in the opening of the first ski lifts in 1972.

Few knew the impact snow would have on this town that had fallen asleep under the steady rocking of popular neglect. Today, Telluride is a desired, almost magical, destination. Mention Telluride and those who know of this tiny mountain gem will raise their eyebrows in appreciation for the almost impossible beauty of the place. "Ah...Telluride," they'll say, "It's paradise."

DINING INTRO

We can all recall a meal that left a permanent impression on our taste buds, that kept us talking about it long after. Most likely, it was not the food alone we recall. We remember the restaurant's atmosphere, the view, or the artful presentation of the elements that comprised the meal. In essence, we retain the sense of magic that comes when food and place flow together seamlessly. In Telluride, where the scenic finery is always dancing before our eyes, the pleasures of food are heightened to their peak.

There's something to be said for a town without a stoplight that can offer the finest cuisine from the far corners of the Earth. At 8,750 feet (higher, if you're dining in the Mountain Village), you can sit and immerse yourself in the culinary cultures of Bavaria, Japan, New Orleans, Provence, Thailand and Tuscany, among others.

Telluride has always possessed a flair for fine food. In the 1890s, the New Sheridan Hotel and the original Cosmopolitan (a self-described "thoroughly first-class resort in every particular") offered the finest French cuisine and wines. Famous throughout Colorado for its imaginative menu, the Sheridan featured turn-of-the-century delicacies such as possum and bear alongside seafood, pork tenderloin, vichyssoise, fresh strawberries and an impressive array of wines from Europe and California.

The chefs of late 20th century Telluride take just as much pride in their craft. Each of the recipes in this book represents countless hours of experimentation and refinement on the parts of the contributors. The hope is that the stories of Telluride's many colorful restauranteurs and the accompanying recipes will provide you with yet another memorable taste of Telluride. Look up to the mountains and enjoy.

-Michelle Kodis

Catch and release on the San Miguel

HIGH ALTITUDE TO LOW ALTITUDE
BAKING CONVERSION

The Telluride Cookbook is a bit unusual in that the recipes are designed for an altitude of 8,750 feet. However, the only recipes that will be affected are ones for baked goods which call for baking powder or baking soda. Recipes containing yeast are not affected. Also, cookie recipes should generally be alright as written since they rely less on the rising affects of baking powder and soda. Cakes and muffins will need some minor changes. For low altitude baking there are just four adjustments one needs to make.

1.   Decrease flour by about 2 teaspoons per cup.

2.   Increase baking powder and baking soda by 25% or 1/4 teaspoon per teaspoon used.

3.   Increase sugar by 2 to 3 tablespoons per cup. Take into account the amount of sugar called for in the recipe when varying it. For a sweet recipe, you may not need to increase the sugar at all, while in a less sweet recipe, you may want to add a full 2 to 3 tablespoons per cup.

4.   As liquid evaporates at a higher rate in high, dry climates, high altitude recipes generally call for an additional 2 to 3 tablespoons of liquid per cup. Start with 2 to 3 tablespoons per cup less than called and then add more if needed.

Recipes that might benefit from an adjustment to lower altitudes (below 5,000 feet) are marked with this icon...

Alta Lakes Mine Remnants

BARCLAY'S

Barclay Daranyi
728-6006

BARCLAY DARANYI

Barclay Daranyi is something of a Bo Jackson or Neon Deion Sanders of the kitchen; a person who loves many professions and is too talented to pursue just one. A part-time chef since high school, Daranyi grew up cooking for extra money during vacations. During her senior year of high school, she made baklava and cheesecakes at a deli. In college, she worked in the dining hall and spent summers baking bread on her parents organic farm in Massachusetts. After graduating from Yale with a degree in painting, Daranyi took a job teaching art at a prep school.

One year, she thought it would be fun to spend the summer cooking at the Skyline Ranch above Telluride and, like so many residents, never left. For the last six years, Daranyi has been a part-time pastry chef at La Marmotte, splitting time between the restaurant, her art studio and her family. In her few spare minutes she bakes wedding and birthday cakes. All of her business is by word-of-mouth and she will not do more than one wedding cake in a weekend.

Still, her reputation has made the rounds. Five days before "the wedding" of 1995, Christy Brinkley's assistant called and asked Daranyi to bake the cake for the supermodel's nuptials. "A lot more went into the exterior of that cake than the interior," she recalls. "I spent most of the time making costumes for the figurines that went on top. Making tiny skis and ski poles out of wood and sewing little cloth ski outfits."

Besides cakes, Daranyi specializes in Indian food, for which she acquired a taste while living in India between the ages of three and five. "My parents used to bribe us with Indian food when we were kids: go to church or clean your room and we'd get Indian food. My parents still go there often and I've kept my love for it ever since."

DAL
(SPICED LENTILS)

SERVES 4

8	oz. lentils
½	teaspoon turmeric
salt to taste	
2	tablespoons butter or ghee (clarified butter)
1	medium onion, finely chopped
¼	teaspoon cayenne pepper
1	teaspoon finely grated fresh ginger

Wash the lentils. Put the lentils, turmeric and 4 pints of water in a saucepan and bring to a boil. Lower the heat, add salt, cover and simmer gently until the lentils are soft. Stir until well mixed.

In a frying pan, heat the butter or ghee and fry the onions. When the onions are soft, add the cayenne and ginger. Mix the onions and spices into the lentils and simmer over low heat until ready to serve.

CHICKEN CURRY

One of my favorite chicken curries. The flavors of cinnamon and cilantro are unbeatable and the coconut milk gives the dish a rich, creamy sauce. A great recipe to expand for a large dinner party.

SERVES 6

⅔	cup chopped onion
5	large garlic cloves
2	tablespoons chopped fresh ginger
1	tablespoon curry powder
1	tablespoon cinnamon
¾	teaspoon dried, crushed red pepper flakes (more if you like your curry hot!)
1	teaspoon coriander
½	cup chopped fresh cilantro
12	chicken thighs
2	tablespoons ghee or vegetable oil
2	cups canned unsweetened coconut milk
1	cup canned chicken broth
½	teaspoon turmeric

In a food processor or blender, blend to a paste the first 7 ingredients and ¼ cup of cilantro, stopping frequently to scrape down the sides of the bowl. Rub the paste over the chicken.

Heat ghee in a large heavy skillet over medium. Add the chicken and brown on all sides; about 6 minutes. Add the coconut milk, broth and turmeric. Reduce the heat, cover and simmer until the chicken is cooked through, turning once; about 30 minutes. Transfer the chicken to a plate.

Boil the liquid in the skillet until reduced to a sauce consistency; about 4 minutes. Season with salt. Return chicken to the skillet and heat through. Sprinkle with the remaining ¼ cup of cilantro. Serve over rice, accompanied by Dal.

CHOCOLATE LOVER'S CAKE

"People are always complaining to me about how hard it is to bake a cake at this altitude (8,750 feet). Here's a recipe I've modified and had great success with."

1½	cups plus 2 tablespoons flour
⅔	cup cocoa powder
1	teaspoon baking soda
¾	teaspoon baking powder
¼	teaspoon salt
1	cup butter (2 sticks)
1¼	cups brown sugar
2	large eggs
2	teaspoons vanilla
¾	cup plus 3 tablespoons buttermilk

Combine the dry ingredients and set aside.

Cream the butter and sugar until light in color. Add the eggs one at a time to the butter and sugar mixture. Add the vanilla.

Alternate mixing the dry ingredients and the buttermilk into the butter, mixing well after each addition.

Pour into two, well-greased and floured circular 8" pans. Bake at 350° for 25 to 30 minutes.

High Altitude Recipe: Refer to page 12

CHOCOLATE CHOCOLATE CHIP COOKIES

Outrageously sinful and delicious cookies!

1	cup butter (2 sticks)
1	cup sugar
½	cup brown sugar
1	egg
1	teaspoon vanilla
1¾	cups plus 2 tablespoons flour
1	teaspoon baking soda
⅔	cup cocoa
2	tablespoons milk
1	cup chopped pecans or walnuts
1½	cups chocolate chips

Cream butter and sugar together. Add the egg and vanilla. Mix in the dry ingredients and the milk. Stir in the nuts and chocolate chips. Place spoonfuls of dough well apart on a greased cookie sheet. Bake at 375° for 10 to 15 minutes.

High Altitude Recipe: Refer to page 12

Owners: Vincent & Joline Esposito
435 West Pacific Street
728-6190

CAMPAGNA

Upon entering Campagna, Telluride's Tuscan restaurant, one is immediately transported to another time, another country. The tables really say it all. Crafted from local pine, they are kindly underwhelming, a perfect complement to the splendid food they hold.

Campagna's owners, Vincent and Joline Esposito, placed their popular restaurant in an old, Dutch Neocolonial on Pacific Street, away from the busy sidewalks of Colorado Avenue, Telluride's main thoroughfare. "We feel we have a more intimate setting here than on Main Street," says Joline Esposito. "We do a good deal of business via word of mouth. People go out of their way to find us."

And for good reason. Specializing in food from the Central Italian region of Tuscany, Chef Vincent's creations have garnered rave reviews from people the world over. The key to Tuscan cooking is freshness," Vincent explains. "You take the best ingredient and capture its essence. If you don't use the best ingredients, the food will not excite you." Indeed, an Italian visitor who dined at Campagna told Vincent, "Your tortelli are like my mama used to make." Can there be a better compliment than that?

Campagna's menu, which changes nightly, is a study in simple but memorable food. One of the most popular dishes is Agnello Arrosto, a New Zealand rack of baby lamb roasted with fresh rosemary. Wild boar is in demand, as is the traditional panzanella, a Tuscan bread salad of tomato and red onion served on a roasted sweet pepper. The menu also includes Risotto ai Funghi (Italian Arborio rice simmered with fresh wild chanterelle, black trumpet and oyster mushrooms) and handmade cheese tortelli topped with butter and fresh sage.

INSALATA DI FAGIOLI CON ARUGULA
BEAN & ARUGULA SALAD

SERVES 4

THE BEANS:

2	cups dried cannellini beans or great white northern beans
1	carrot
1	bulb garlic
8	large fresh sage leaves
¼	rib celery
¼	teaspoon black pepper
½	cup of very good extra-virgin olive oil

This recipe should be started 2 days before you serve it.

Soak the beans in water to cover by double for 24 hours. Drain the beans and rinse well.

Place the beans in a large pot (with plenty of room for the beans to grow) with fresh water to cover by 1" - 2". Add the rest of the ingredients (unchopped). Cook uncovered at medium-high heat, keeping the liquid at a high simmer. Add more water as needed.

When the beans are about 30 minutes from being done (total cooking time should be 2-3 hours, depending on the freshness of the dried beans), add one tablespoon of sea salt. Reduce heat to a slow simmer. Do not add any more water unless the beans are about to dry out. They should swim in the liquid at this point, not drown.

When the beans are soft and cooked through (but not mush!), take them off the heat and cool overnight.

THE SALAD:

1   small red onion, chopped roughly
2   tablespoons chopped Italian parsley (flat leaf parsley)
1   large pinch sea salt
fresh ground black pepper to taste
Tuscan extra virgin olive oil (oil quality is extremely important)
½   pound fresh young arugula

Drain the cooked beans and discard the carrot, garlic, celery and sage. Rinse the beans briefly with warm water. To the beans, add the onion, parsley, sea salt, ground pepper and enough olive oil to coat. Toss and let sit at room temperature for one hour.

[Note: *Beans can be made ahead to this point and refrigerate for up to one day. Remember to bring them back to room temperature before serving.*]

Spoon the bean salad onto a large bed of fresh, young arugula. Garnish with a few thin strips of soft sundried tomato. Serve with a drizzle of extra virgin olive oil at the table.

TORTELLI DI VITELLO
(TUSCAN RAVIOLI MADE WITH FRESH PASTA & A VEAL FILLING)

SERVES 4

THE PASTA:

3	eggs
1	egg yolk
1	teaspoon olive oil

pinch of salt

2	cups (approximately) all-purpose flour

Mix the eggs, yolk, olive oil and salt in a food processor with a metal blade. Add the flour and continue mixing until it all comes together in a ball (the amount of flour can vary a little depending on the size of the eggs and the dampness of the flour). Remove the pasta ball and knead until elastic and smooth. Wrap in plastic and let sit for one hour at room temperature.

THE FILLING *(can be made up to a day ahead and refrigerated)*:

1½	pounds roasted veal
	(any lean cut such as a shoulder roast will do) [See Note]
¾	pound Swiss chard
¾	cup fresh fine bread crumbs
	(quickly grind stale bread in a food processor)

large pinch nutmeg

½	cup grated Parmigiano-Reggiano
2	eggs
¼	cup chopped fresh Italian parsley (flat leaf parsley)
2	tablespoons chopped fresh sage

salt and pepper to taste

[Note: *The veal must first be roasted in the oven: season with olive oil, salt, black pepper and chopped, fresh garlic and sage. Cool in the refrigerator. A good idea would be to make a three pound roast the day before, eat half and use the left-overs for the tortelli. Alternatively, you can purchase ground veal or even turkey and cook it with a little garlic and olive oil before using it as the filling.*]

Thoroughly wash the Swiss chard in cool water to remove any dirt. Remove the stalks. Place the wet chard in a covered saute/frying pan at high heat to steam (no additional water is necessary). This should take only a few minutes. Thoroughly drain the chard and squeeze out the excess water. Cool in the refrigerator.

Trim any major pieces of fat from the roasted veal and chop in a food processor (with a metal blade) until slightly course. Add the cooked Swiss chard and process until fine. Empty the mixture into a bowl and stir in the other ingredients. Mix well.

ASSEMBLING THE TORTELLI:

Using a manual pasta rolling machine, roll out half the dough until very thin. Lay a rectangular sheet of pasta onto a lightly flour-dusted surface. Spoon small balls of the filling onto half the length of the sheet, two across, about 3" apart. Do this to only half the length of the sheet, as the other half will be folded over to form the top of the tortelli. Before folding, spray the pasta lightly with water so the two halves will stick and seal. Fold over and press the edges together.

Using a ravioli cutter wheel or knife, cut the square tortelli shapes from the filled pasta sheet (if using a knife, seal the edges of each tortelli with your fingers). Place on floured wax paper. If you are not cooking right away, cover with plastic wrap and refrigerate (they will only keep for a few hours, however). Repeat with the other half of the pasta.

COOKING THE TORTELLI:

Bring a large pot of salted water to a boil. Add the tortelli and cook until just tender; about 3-4 minutes (try one).

THE BUTTER SAUCE:

4   tablespoons unsalted butter at room temperature or warmer,
       cut into small pieces
fresh whole sage leaves, about 16 large or more smaller ones
a very small pinch of salt
a grind or two of black pepper

Place all of the ingredients in a warm bowl and mix. Add the cooked tortelli and toss together. Serve with a light sprinkling of grated Parmigiano-Reggiano and a fresh sage leaf garnish.

Paragliding above the San Juans

FRUTTI MISTI DI BOSCO
(BROILED FRUIT WITH ZABAGLIONE)

SERVES 4

2-3   cups mixed berries (strawberries, blackberries, raspberries
       and blueberries) and fresh peach wedges if available
4   teaspoons chopped walnuts

Preheat the broiler. Arrange the fruit in individual oven-proof dishes.

THE ZABAGLIONE:

4   egg yolks
3   tablespoons sugar
1   tablespoon Marsala wine or other sweet dessert wine

Mix yolks, sugar and wine in a metal bowl over a pot of boiling water that was just turned off. Mix with a whisk until thick and frothy.

Drizzle 4 or 5 tablespoons of zabaglione over each dish of fruit. Sprinkle with chopped walnuts. Place under the broiler until golden (watch closely!). Serve immediately.

Cosmopolitan *Hotel Columbia*

Owner: Chad Scothorn
300 West San Juan Avenue
728-1292

COSMOPOLITAN

In recent years, Telluride has become home to many famous actors, musicians and novelists. The fall of 1995 saw the arrival of a new type of star, Telluride's first celebrity chef, Chad Scothorn. Scothorn moved to Telluride to open the Cosmopolitan restaurant in the Columbia Hotel at the bottom of gondola and the Oak Street Lift. Scothorn and the Columbia's owners, Jeff Campbell and Jim Lincoln, were introduced by local baker extraordinaire Cindy Farny, with whom Scothorn went to dessert and bread school in France.

Before meeting Campbell and Lincoln, Scothorn was the owner of Chadwick's in Vail, which received mention in *The New York Times* and *Town and Country Magazine.* Prior to that, he ran Beaver Creek's acclaimed on-mountain Beano's Cabin, which was covered in *Bon Appetit, Snow Country* and *Connoisseur* and was featured as one of *Esquire Magazine's* Top 100 New Restaurants.

Scothorn started cooking at the of 14, and, he says, "Before I graduated from high school, I was running a kitchen." After majoring in hotel and restaurant management, he realized that his true love was cooking and enrolled at the Culinary Institute of America. With his reputation, Scothorn could make several times as much money running a restaurant in a big city, but, he says, "I just love living in the mountains. I love to ski and cross-country ski and snowshoe. Plus, it's great living somewhere where people know you."

The Cosmopolitan features "creative American cuisine," serving three meals a day. There will be plenty of healthy choices and fresh fish on the menu, but Scothorn promises that "we'll always have a red meat as well." One of Scothorn's signatures is in-house smoking and highlights of his ever-changing menu include roasted veal tenderloin with shiitake mushrooms and lemon grass, and a house-smoked duck with barley risotto.

MUSSEL SOUP WITH FRESH BASIL & GARLIC BREAD

SERVES 6

48	mussels, alive and cleaned
48	oz. can tomatoes whole in juice
2	tablespoons minced garlic
1	teaspoon crushed red pepper
1	tablespoon olive oil
4	oz. dry white wine
2	oz. Asiago cheese, thinly sliced
½	cup fresh basil, thinly sliced

garlic bread (see below)

Clean and debeard the mussels. Set aside.

In a soup pot, saute the garlic and red pepper in olive oil. Hand crush the tomatoes (do not used crushed in the can tomatoes as they are in puree rather than juice and lend the wrong consistency to the soup). Add the tomatoes and white wine. Simmer for 5 minutes. Taste for salt and pepper (go light on the salt as the cheese and mussels can add some saltiness later).

At this time, the soup should appear very thin. If it doesn't, thin it with canned or bottled clam juice (or water).

Over medium-high heat, add the mussels and cover the pot. Shake the pot a little with the lid on (like popcorn), this will encourage the mussels to open sooner. Check the mussels after 4-5 minutes. When they open, they are ready.

Portion the soup into 6 large bowls. Garnish with Asiago, basil and garlic bread.

THE GARLIC BREAD:

1	baguette, cut into ½" thick slices
1	tablespoon olive oil
1	teaspoon minced garlic

Heat the olive oil with the garlic. Brush the baguette slices with the oil and toast on a char-broiler or in a hot oven.

SEARED SALMON WITH
TRUFFLE VINAIGRETTE

SERVES 6

2   pounds salmon fillet, boned and paillard [see note]
1   pound asparagus spears, blanched
2   pounds red potatoes, boiled and cooled
Truffle Vinaigrette (see recipe below)

Prepare the char-broiler (hot).

While one person is preparing the salmon, another should prepare the asparagus and potatoes.

Slice the potatoes into ½ inch thick rounds. Toss the potatoes and asparagus with a small amount of olive oil and grill lightly.

Lightly season the salmon fillets with salt and white pepper. Pre-heat a non-stick pan, then sear the salmon on high heat on both sides so that it is slightly rare in the middle and brown on the outside. This will take 1-2 minutes if the pan is hot enough. Do not over-crowd the pan. Use more than one pan if necessary or cook the salmon in batches.

To serve, place 5-6 grilled potato rounds in the center of each plate. Place the salmon atop the potatoes. Prop 5-6 asparagus spears half on the salmon, half on the plate to give the presentation some vertical contrast. Ladle 2 oz. of vinaigrette over the salmon.

[Note: *Paillard is a French term for a cut of chicken or meat. In this case, when trimming the salmon, cut the entire fillet horizontally with a very sharp knife. This will result in two, very long, thin pieces of salmon. Now cut 6 portions - this will yield a large-looking portion which will cook very quickly.*]

TRUFFLE VINAIGRETTE:

½   cup Champagne vinegar
½   cup truffle peelings (available at specialty food stores)
1½   cups olive oil
salt and white pepper to taste

Combine the vinegar and truffle peelings. Slowly whisk in the olive oil and season with salt and white pepper.

CHOCOLATE HAZELNUT PUDDING WITH BOURBON WHIPPED CREAM

SERVES 6

3	oz. bread (approx. 6 slices), diced
½	cup whipping cream
3	oz. bittersweet or semisweet chocolate
½	cup hazelnuts, roasted, skinned and chopped
½	cup sugar
4	tablespoons butter
3	eggs, separated

Preheat the oven to 375°.

Butter 6 small souffle molds or one 3-4 cup casserole dish.

Soak the diced bread in the cream for 30 minutes.

Melt the chocolate in a double boiler.

Beat the butter and egg yolks. Add the melted chocolate, hazelnuts, bread and ¼ cup of sugar. Mix well.

Make a meringue by whipping the egg whites until soft peaks form. Next, add the remaining ¼ cup of sugar and beat until stiff. Fold the whites into the chocolate mixture. Pour into the molds or casserole and bake for 45 minutes or until done (set and firm, not loose and runny).

Serve with sweetened whipped cream to which a small amount of bourbon has been added.

The Historic San Miguel County Courthouse

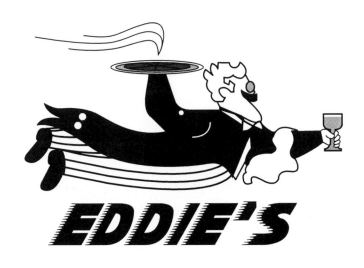

Eddie Snyder
300 West Colorado Avenue
728-5335

EDDIE'S

Eddie's is Telluride's answer to the pizza craving and people follow their noses to this popular eatery with one thing in mind: a hot slice. At Eddie's, plain old cheese and pepperoni share menu space with exotics such as the Dosie Doe, a Dadaist concoction of roasted garlic, sun-dried tomatoes, olive oil, scallions, parsley, Gorgonzola, mozzarella and Parmesan cheeses, and a hint of marinara sauce.

Eddie's has been serving an extensive lunch and dinner menu for eight years. While the restaurant is best-known for its specialty pizzas, diners have a variety of Italian options. There is the mixed seafood grill (swordfish, halibut and salmon marinated, grilled and served with fettuccini in a feta-dill sauce); Tuna Parisian (two grilled yellowfin tuna fillets served with linguini in a sauce of lemon, white wine and Worcestershire); and basil pesto (homemade pesto tossed with linguini and served with grilled chicken or tuna).

The dining room's open floor plan offers a fun, casual atmosphere, while the deck, overlooking Elk's Park and sporting epic views of the end of the canyon, is a great place to lunch or relax in the early evening and try one of Eddie's microbrews, including their famous Raspberry Wheat.

GREEN CHILE CORN CHOWDER

SERVES 4

2	16 oz. cans corn, drained
2	4 oz. cans diced mild green chiles
1	cup diced onion
1	cup water
2	pinches black pepper
½	teaspoon or more to taste garlic powder or fresh garlic
2	pinches vegetable base
1	quart milk

roux (see below)

In a large pot, add all of the ingredients except the milk. Bring to a boil and simmer for 10 minutes. Turn off the heat and add the milk. Gradually stir in small amounts of roux until the desired thickness is reached. Heat on low until ready to serve. Garnish with cilantro sprig.

Add tomatillos (green tomatoes) or roasted red peppers for more flavor or varied taste.

THE ROUX:

Melt 4 tablespoons of butter in a sauce pan. Slowly stir in 4 tablespoons of flour until a nice, moist paste is achieved.

SHRIMP PARISIAN

SERVES 4

20	16-20 count shrimp, peeled, deveined and butterflied
4	tablespoons butter
2	tablespoons minced garlic
1	cup white wine

juice of one lemon

⅛	cup Worcestershire sauce
4	tomatoes, quartered
4	tablespoons breadcrumbs

chopped fresh parsley

Melt the butter in a sauce pan over high heat. Add the garlic and saute very briefly. Add the shrimp and cook for one minute.

Deglaze the pan with the wine. Add the lemon juice and Worcestershire. Flip the shrimp and let cook until just pink on both sides. Remove the shrimp so they don't over-cook.

Add the tomatoes and bread crumbs. Once the tomatoes are hot, remove them from the pan. Add the chopped parsley to the sauce and toss with linguini.

Place linguini in center of each plate and alternate tomato wedges and shrimp around the outside.

CHICKEN D'ADAMO

SERVES 4

4	boneless chicken breasts
6	tablespoons butter
1	cup sliced mushrooms
1	teaspoon minced garlic
9	tablespoons crumbled Feta cheese
1	cup white wine
1	cup heavy whipping cream
⅔	cup artichoke hearts, quartered
⅔	cup pitted black olives, sliced

Pound chicken breasts until even and thin. Coat both sides of each breast with flour. Heat the oil in saute pan over high heat. Once the oil is hot, sear the chicken (don't burn yourself). Flip the chicken so each side is almost crispy. Drain the oil.

Reduce the heat to medium, add the butter, mushrooms, garlic and Feta. Cook until the butter is absorbed by the mushrooms. Deglaze with the wine, letting the alcohol burn off, the mushrooms soften and the Feta melt.

Add the cream and stir so the Feta doesn't stick to the pan. Add the artichoke hearts and olives. Let the sauce reduce and thicken; about 2-3 minutes. Don't overcook the sauce as it will separate. Turn down the heat if necessary. Finish with chopped fresh basil leaves and pour over linguini.

HOT FUDGE KAHLUA CAKE

1	cup all-purpose flour
¾	cup sugar
4	tablespoons cocoa
2	teaspoons cinnamon
2	teaspoons baking powder
¼	teaspoon salt
½	cup milk
½	cup Kahlua
3	tablespoons butter, melted
1	cup brown sugar
½	cup cocoa
2	cups boiling water

Stir together the first six ingredients in an ungreased 8" square pan. Add the milk, Kahlua and melted butter and stir well.

In a small bowl, mix the brown sugar and the ½ cup of cocoa. Sprinkle this over the dough mix in the square pan. Do not stir!

Pour the boiling water over the top of the mixture. Stir two times only. Bake at 350° for 35 minutes, or until cake is set and the pudding is bubbling.

Best served hot!

Owner/Chef: Charles R. H. Moore
646 Mountain Village Boulevard
Mountain Village
728-9717

EVANGELINE'S

Just six weeks after opening its discreet doors in September 1991, Evangeline's received its literary coming-out party in the *New York Times,* which warmly welcomed the high-altitude newcomer to the restaurant scene. Managed by chef/owner Chas Moore, Evangeline's seats a cozy 35 in an atmosphere redolent of the colors and feel of New Orleans. Borrowing its name from the epic Longfellow poem, Evangeline's specializes in the Creole cuisine of New Orleans with an underlying influence of the foods and flavors of Provence.

Moore notes that the twin passions of New Orleans are music and food and that there is considerable correlation between them. "They are the two passions of my life," he says. "Like much of the music I love, my cooking is improvisational, for we change our menu every night. We have recipes, like sheet music, but we believe that spontaneity is a critical element. Thus, when following these recipes, you are asked to never lose sight of your own internal muse. Great cooking must flow from the soul and have an element of the individual."

Evangeline's menu is pleasingly easy to navigate. Each night, Chef Moore offers a selection of three appetizers, four entrees and three desserts. Popular menu items include handmade ravioli stuffed with ricotta cheese, crab meat and herbs, tossed in a crawfish sauce; grilled fillet of escolar in a red onion sauce served with roasted yams and sauteed spinach; the John Wayne cowboy steak (a grilled, bone-in ribeye topped with garlic oil and red wine sauce, served with mashed potatoes and mushrooms) and pasta crusted salmon (sauteed pasta and crusted fillet of salmon served in a roasted vegetable sauce). Desserts reflect Moore's extensive experience as a pastry chef. They are simple but spectacular, particularly the filo cup filled with fresh wild strawberries and served with creme fraiche and caramel.

SHRIMP CREOLE

SERVES 4

CREOLE SAUCE:

1	cup coarsely diced onion
2	tablespoons butter
1	cup coarsely diced celery
½	cup coarsely diced bell pepper
1	tablespoon chopped garlic
¾	tablespoon Cajun seasoning (recipe follows)
⅓	cup tomato paste
1½	cups crushed tomatoes
2	cups water
1¼	teaspoons black pepper
1	whole bay leaf
1½	teaspoons Crystal Hot Sauce

"Before starting any recipe, it is important to set out all of the ingredients. This is probably the most important thing I learned studying pastry in France.

Creole sauce is the classic New Orleans sauce. Although Creole cooking is more refined than Cajun, this is still a hearty sauce. Thus, the cut vegetables should be coarse, about the size of one's fingernail.

First, melt the butter and then caramelize the onion. The onion should be nice and brown so that the caramelizing sugar sweetens the final sauce. Next, add the celery, bell pepper, garlic and Cajun seasoning. Be sure not to over-cook the vegetables as they should retain a certain crunch. Add the rest of the ingredients, bring to a boil and let simmer on a low heat for 30 minutes.

This sauce can be made in advance, and, actually, it is preferable to do so as all tomato-based sauces improve after one day.

At the restaurant, all of my recipes end with "label, date and refrigerate." According to the health code, all food items must be clearly identified, and after having looked in too many friends' refrigerators and freezers, I feel that this is always a good policy."

THE SHRIMP:

7	21/25 count shrimp per person
½	cup cooked rice per person
1	tablespoon butter per person
¾	cup Creole sauce per person

"Sprinkle the shrimp with Cajun seasoning to taste and saute them in butter. I am constantly amazed how much some restaurants cook shrimp. One only has to cook them until they are lightly pink on both sides. Add about ¾ cup of Creole sauce per serving. Heat until warm and serve over rice.

I have found that what normally separates dining out and eating in is presentation. At Evangeline's, when we come up with an exceptionally attractive dish, it will always out-sell the others. This is because one does eat with one's eyes.

Arrange the rice in a circle around the edge of the plate. Then place six shrimp atop the rice and one in the center. To finish, ladle the sauce into the center and top with slices of green onion."

CAJUN SEASONING:

2	tablespoons salt
1½	teaspoons granulated garlic
1½	teaspoons black pepper
1¼	teaspoons cayenne pepper
¾	teaspoon cumin
¾	teaspoon paprika
1¼	teaspoons granulated onion

"Many, if not most, Cajun seasonings I have tried are either too salty or have too much cayenne. This recipe brings out just the right combination of tastes. Simply measure out the ingredients and blend them together. Try not to breathe too deeply and cough on the pepper filling the air."

Rated #1 for scenery by Snow Country *magazine*

COBBLER DE MON FRERE DIEGO

SERVES 12

One of the greatest joys of owning a restaurant is the friendships you develop with your customers. One of my best customers, who has become such a good friend that I am honored to call him my brother, is a man named Diego Veitia. He always used to come in for dinner and order Stilton cheese with his port. I decided to make him a special dessert with Stilton already in it.

THE SHORTCAKE:

3	cups flour
¼	cup sugar
1	tablespoon baking powder
1	teaspoon salt
10	tablespoons butter, pre-softened
1	cup heavy cream

Blend the dry ingredients in a mixer. Cut the butter into mixer. Once incorporated, pour in the cream and continue to mix until just blended. Turn out onto a floured counter. Roll out the dough to fit in a 9" x 11" baking pan. Bake at 350° until golden brown, about 20 minutes.

THE FILLING:

10	Granny Smith apples
4	tablespoons butter
½	cup brown sugar
1	tablespoon cinnamon
1	teaspoon nutmeg

While the shortcake is baking, slice the apples and saute until soft. Mix the apples with the butter, brown sugar and spices. Place in a colander and let drain.

Continued on page 46

THE TOPPING:

1	cup flour
⅝	cup brown sugar
½	cup sugar
4	tablespoons butter
4	oz. Stilton cheese

Place the flour and sugars in a mixer and blend. Cut the butter into small cubes and mix into the dry ingredients until the mixture reaches a crumbly consistency. DO NOT OVERMIX. Crumble in the cheese and mix until it is well combined but still chunky.

Remove the pan with the shortcake bottom and cover with the sauteed apples. Then cover with the topping and bake at 350° until golden brown, about 20 to 30 minutes.

The Ophir Needles

Owners: Jake Linzinmeir & Elaine Palminteri
200 West Colorado Avenue
728-4250

THE EXCELSIOR CAFE

The building housing the Excelsior Cafe is a true Telluride local. Located on the corner of Colorado Avenue and Fir Street, the Excelsior has housed the Thomkins & Christie hardware store, a bowling alley, an art gallery and offices, a sure indication of the constantly changing face of Telluride.

The Excelsior has continually gained in popularity under the careful guidance of owners Jake Linzinmeir and Elaine Palminteri, who moved to Telluride fresh out of Cornell University's Hotel and Restaurant Management School. Upon buying the restaurant, their first task was to make the book as attractive as its classic red brick cover. They remodeled extensively, installing a copper counter and decorating the bistro with skylights, simple wooden tables and paintings by local artists. The restaurant now sports a casual but elegant style, with simplicity in decor and presentation the key elements of the design.

The food at the Excelsior is described by Linzinmeir as "eclectic nouvelle Italian cuisine." He adds, "We change the menu seasonally, focusing on the lighter foods of southern Italy during the summer and the heartier foods of northern Italy in the winter." Pastas are the most popular offerings, with a creative mix of traditional and not-so-traditional ingredients, such as seared shrimp, fresh tuna, capers, olives and fresh herbs, to name a few.

If you are of the mind that no meal is complete without wine, you will find company at the Excelsior. Here, the wine list, which focuses on Californian and Italian vineyards, gets as much billing as the dinner menu, and Linzinmeir and Palminteri regularly board airplanes in search of new vintages to add to their extensive collection.

FOCACCIA

MAKES 3 LOAVES

3	tablespoons dry yeast
1½	teaspoons salt
1	tablespoon sugar
¼	cup milk
3	cups lukewarm water
½	cup olive oil
7½	cups all-purpose flour
1	cup durham flour (bread flour)
2	teaspoons dried basil (double for fresh herbs)
1	teaspoon dried oregano (double for fresh herbs)

Mix the yeast, salt, sugar, milk and water and let sit for 10-15 minutes. Meanwhile, mix the herbs into the flour. When the yeast mixture begins to bubble, stir and mix it into the bread flour and 5 cups of all-purpose flour.

Knead in the remaining flour until the dough is smooth and elastic. Let it rise until doubled in size.

Roll out the dough to fit in a baking pan that has been brushed with oil. A good option would be to split the dough into thirds and roll it out to fit into three 9" cake pans. Brush top of dough with oil and sprinkle with salt and oregano.

Let rise until double in volume and bake at 375° for 20 minutes or until light brown on top.

Ed. Note: *Any unused portions can be frozen and enjoyed with equal success at a later date by just bringing it to room temperature and then warming it in the oven.*

TOMATO & ASPARAGUS SALAD WITH TOASTED PINE NUT VINAIGRETTE

SERVES 6

TOASTED PINE NUT VINAIGRETTE:

¼	pound pine nuts
¾	cup olive oil
¼	cup white wine vinegar
¼	cup shallots
1½	teaspoons chopped garlic
½	teaspoon salt
¼	teaspoon black pepper

Toast the pine nuts until golden (watch them carefully as they burn easily!). Puree the nuts with oil and vinegar and then stir in the remaining ingredients.

THE SALAD:

6	Roma tomatoes
42	asparagus spears

Peel and hollow the tomatoes. Trim the bottoms off of the asparagus spears and blanch the tips. Stuff each tomato with 7 tips. Top with the pine nut vinaigrette and shaved Parmesan cheese.

ORECCHIETTE AMATRICIANA

SERVES 4 TO 6

¼	pound imported pancetta
2	large red bell peppers
¼	cup fresh oregano
½	cup fresh basil
2	16 oz. boxes orecchiette pasta
4	Roma tomatoes, sliced
1	tablespoon red pepper flakes
1	bunch fresh spinach
2	tablespoons fresh minced garlic
½	cup extra virgin olive oil

white wine to deglaze pan

1	cup pomodoro or tomato sauce
1	cup Parmigiano-Reggiano cheese

Char and peel the red peppers. Seed and slice.

Cook the pasta al dente (firm).

Heat the olive oil with the pancetta in a saute pan until browned. Add the garlic, Roma tomatoes, oregano, roasted red peppers and crushed red pepper. Immediately deglaze the pan with the white wine.

Add the tomato sauce and simmer for one minute. Add the spinach and cook until just wilted. Add the pasta and toss.

Serve with fresh Parmigiano-Reggiano and basil leaves.

Best with a Chianti (Nozzole, Chianti Classico Riserva 1990) or an Italian dry white wine (Bucci, Verdicchio di Jesi, Classico).

TIRA MI SU

SERVES 4

MASCARPONE MOUSSE:

3	egg yolks
6	egg whites
¼	cup sugar
2	pints Mascarpone cheese

COFFEE DIP:

1	pot very strong coffee (half espresso, if possible)
⅛	cup Kahlua or other coffee liqueur
1	package Savoiardi (lady fingers), about one pound

unsweetened cocoa

In a large mixing bowl, whisk the yolks with ⅓ of the sugar until lemon in color. Next, mix in the Mascarpone.

In a second bowl with a beater, whip the egg whites with the second ⅓ of the sugar until stiff but not dry.

In medium mixing bowl, whisk the coffee liqueur and the remaining sugar until the sugar dissolves.

Gently fold the egg yolk mixture into the whipped whites.

Quickly dip each lady finger into the coffee mixture and place in the bottom of a square glass casserole dish until the bottom is covered.

Spread the mascarpone mixture over the soaked lady fingers and smooth it out.

Repeat the coffee dip with the second half of the lady fingers and layer over the mascarpone mixture.

Spread the other half of the mascarpone mixture atop the lady fingers, smooth it out and dust heavily with cocoa. Chill for 3 or more hours.

Owners: Robby O'Dell & Eric Hill
122 South Oak Street
728-3985

FAT ALLEY BBQ

Located in the historic yellow Dahl Haus, a former rooming house, Fat Alley is a rib-lover's dream. Owned by Robby O'Dell (from Alabama) and Eric Hill (from Austin, Texas), Fat Alley features southern favorites such as jambalaya, chicken fried steak, Jamaican jerked chicken, St. Louis pork ribs, beef ribs and hickory smoked brisket.

One of the most popular items is the Carolina Smoked Pork Shoulder, smoked shoulder marinated in vinegar, brown sugar and red pepper, served on a bun with coleslaw over the top. Coleslaw on top? "Yep," says O'Dell with his smooth-as-molasses accent, "that's the way we do it in the South. Elvis would be proud."

Keeping things very, very Southern is one of the priorities of Fat Alley's owners. O'Dell and Hill purchased the eatery in the summer of 1995. They had been working in restaurants in Vail for years when they saw an ad selling Fat Alley. Soon after, they found themselves the owners of one of Telluride's most popular restaurants. They opted not to revamp the menu, but did add a few of their own touches, tweaking the basic barbecue sauce and introducing a Memphis-style sauce, a lighter version with a more pronounced vinegar undertone.

For vegetarians and the cholesterol conscious, the menu includes braised vinaigrette greens, red beans and rice, smoked baked potatoes, snap pea and Feta salad, the ever-popular potato-black bean saute and super, crisp-on-the-outside, soft-on-the-inside French fries.

Tables are decorated with a variety of hot sauces, but if you really want to send your taste buds to another planet, ask for Dave's Insanity hot sauce. You have to request it specially as it's too inflammatory to be left within easy reach.

CAROLINA SMOKED PORK SHOULDER SANDWICH

SERVES 4 TO 6

THE MARINADE:

1	quart white vinegar
2	teaspoons crushed red pepper flakes
½	large white onion
1	cup brown sugar
1	tablespoon lemon juice
6	tablespoons butter
1	tablespoon black pepper
½	teaspoon salt
¼	teaspoon garlic powder or garlic salt

Puree the onion. Place all of the ingredients except the butter in a large sauce pan. Bring to a boil. Stir often to keep the brown sugar from sticking. After boiling for 3 minutes, reduce the heat, add the butter and stir to mix. Keep the marinade refrigerated. Makes one quart.

THE PORK SHOULDER:

Baste 2 pounds of smoked pork shoulder for up to 2 days, rotating it so all sides are marinated. Put the shoulder in a pan and heat. Slice and serve on fresh rolls with coleslaw on top.

ZITI PASTA

SERVES 4 TO 6

⅛	cup olive oil
1	medium onion, diced
2	stalks celery, diced
4	Anaheim chile peppers, seeded and sliced into rings
½	bunch cilantro
1	tablespoon chopped garlic
1	cup water
2	tablespoons chili powder
1	tablespoon cumin
1	teaspoon salt
1	package frozen spinach, thawed
2	16 oz. cans black beans
1	16 oz. package penne pasta

Heat the oil and saute the onion, celery and chile pepper until tender. Add the seasonings, spinach and water. Allow to cool, then add the beans.

Cook the pasta until al dente. Reheat the spinach and beans and add the pasta. Finish with Parmesan cheese.

Owners: Howie & Lois Stern
103 West Colorado Avenue
728-3888

FLORADORA

How did an urban studies major from Philadelphia and a peace-preaching 60s flowerchild come to own one of Telluride's oldest restaurants? "It's simple," says Lois Stern, of the Howie-and-Lois, husband-and-wife team that owns the Floradora. "We came to learn to ski, back when Telluride didn't even have a ski lift. We got jobs at this restaurant called the Floradora. I waited tables. Howie washed dishes and worked his way up to manager. Now we own the place."

Call it the Telluride Dream. Deciding that an ideal life would include the constant company of breathtaking mountains, the Sterns (Lois was the student, Howie the Bronx, N.Y.-born activist who made his own health foods in the early 70s) bought the Floradora in 1977.

The menu includes hand-cut steaks, fresh seafood, pasta, a salad bar, fajitas and creatively-named burgers such as the Rattlesnake Burger (a combination of chorizo and ground beef). Lois especially recommends the blackened salmon served on organic greens; the Thai chicken pasta; and the chicken fried steak served with mashed potatoes and gravy.

Decorated with pennants from sports teams of every affiliation and locale, the restaurant is part cozy booths, part sports bar with numerous televisions tuned to the game of the moment at all times. The Floradora is often crowded, but waits are short and orders taken promptly. Plus, you get one of the best greetings in town from Howie, who meets you at the door with his one-of-a-kind "How many are we, kids?" Now that's service.

THAI CHICKEN SALAD

SERVES 4

GINGERED PEANUT DRESSING:

⅛	pound peanuts
⅓	cup rice vinegar
1-1½	tablespoons Dijon mustard
2	tablespoons soy sauce
⅛	teaspoon grated fresh ginger root (to taste)
1	clove garlic, chopped
1½	tablespoons sugar
1	cup vegetable oil
⅛	cup sesame oil
¼	teaspoon crushed red pepper
⅛-½	teaspoon cayenne pepper

In a bowl, combine the vinegar and mustard. In a blender, combine the soy sauce, garlic and ginger. Blend well. Add to the vinegar and mustard. Then add the sugar, oils, cayenne and crushed red peppers. Stir well. Crush the peanuts in the blender and stir into the dressing.

THE SALAD:

2 pounds grilled chicken breast (4 boneless breasts)
rice noodles
tomato wedges
cucumber slices
peeled, sliced kiwi
sliced roasted red pepper
organic greens

Pour approximately 3 oz. of dressing over the organic greens. Top with rice noodles. Arrange the tomatoes, cucumber, kiwi and sliced chicken breast on top. Garnish with the roasted red pepper.

BLACKENED SALMON ON ORGANIC GREENS WITH CAJUN VINAIGRETTE DRESSING

SERVES 4

CAJUN VINAIGRETTE:
½   cup white vinegar
1   cup olive oil
Cajun seasoning (1 to 2 teaspoons, to taste)
1½   teaspoons cayenne pepper
½   teaspoon thyme
1½   tablespoons sugar
3   oz. mandarin oranges
1½   teaspoons Dijon mustard

Blend all of the vinaigrette ingredients at high speed. Let stand in the refrigerator for one hour.

THE SALMON:
4   fresh 8 oz. salmon fillets
Cajun seasoning
organic greens

Dust both sides of the salmon fillets with Cajun seasoning. Grill or broil until both sides are done (time depends on thickness).

Arrange the salmon on a platter covered with the greens. Drizzle with the vinaigrette.

SIRLOIN STEAK WITH
BRANDIED GREEN PEPPERCORNS

SERVES 4

4	8 oz. hand-cut sirloin steaks (or filet mignon)
8	oz. demi glaze (or substitute beef stock)
1	clove garlic
1	bay leaf
½	cup brandy
2	tablespoons green peppercorns
¼	cup heavy cream

salt and pepper

Cook the demi glaze, garlic and bay leaf over low heat until reduced to about ½ cup. Add the brandy and peppercorns. Cook until the mixture is reduced to ¾ cup.

Remove the bay leaf and garlic. Add the cream and cook until blended. Add salt and pepper to taste.

Cook the steaks to desired temperature. To serve, pour approximately 2 tablespoons of sauce over each steak.

The San Juan backcountry - a snowboarder's eden

Owners: Honga Im & Daisuke Utagawa
138 East Colorado Avenue
728-5134

HONGA'S LOTUS PETAL

Korean-born Honga Im named her restaurant after the lotus petal, the Buddhist representation of enlightenment. "Buddha's philosophy is important, particularly as it relates to a love of nature," Says Im. "I translate that philosophy into my cooking, respecting the lives of the animals and appreciating the plants. We recycle, precycle and buy meats and poultry that are free of chemicals and hormones. When possible, we use regionally grown produce and try very hard to be an environmentally low-impact restaurant."

Honga's specializes in foods of the Pacific Rim, including Bali, Japan, Korea and Thailand. One of the restaurant's most popular features is its greenhouse dining area, a lofty, bright space with a tile floor and round tables in which to partake in the Lotus Petal magic. The interior dining room, with its red walls, abundance of fresh flowers and hanging paper lanterns, is a step out of the Telluride mountains into the Orient.

Asian cooking is marked by the variety of flavors that lie hidden in layers in the food, surfacing in steps. Soy sauce, honey, cilantro, lemon grass, fish sauce, garlic, ginger and sesame oil are Im's favorites, and she combines them in artful ways to create memorable food. She prepares the food to order, using only the freshest ingredients. This method, she says, retains the food's 'chi,' or energy. Chi is lost when foods are prepared ahead and added later.

Honga's menu includes pad thai, blackened tofu, pot stickers, miso soup, som tam (spicy cucumber salad) and pineapple bamboo curry. The full sushi bar features such exotics as tako (octopus), tobiko (flying fish roe) and ama ebi (fresh sweet shrimp), as well as the more standard California Rolls, salmon and tuna. For dessert, don't miss the Banana Delight, fried bananas topped with ice cream, fresh fruit, chocolate sauce, almonds and "lots of love."

TOM YAM SOUP
(LEMON GRASS SOUP)

SERVES 4

5	cups shrimp stock
1	stalk lemon grass
3	cloves garlic, minced
2	lemons, juiced
½	cup fish sauce
1	tomato
½	cup rock shrimp, peeled
1	stalk celery
¼	cup cilantro
black pepper	
1	jalapeno, seeded and sliced into horizontal rings
½	cup bamboo shoots

Make the shrimp stock by boiling shrimp shells in water or by just cooking the rock shrimp and reserving the water as the stock.

Bring the stock to a boil and add diagonally cut lemon grass. Then add the garlic, lemon juice, fish sauce, diced tomato, diagonally cut celery, bamboo shoots and rock shrimp. Finally, add the jalapeno rings and black pepper to taste. Simmer for 10 minutes. Ladle into bowls and top with fresh cilantro.

Great for colds and winter warmth.

TOFU WITH MIXED VEGETABLES

SERVES 4

1	pound hard tofu
2	broccoli trees
5	shiitake mushrooms, without stems
1	red bell pepper
1	carrot
1	medium onion
2	arms bok choy
1	cup bean sprouts
3	cloves garlic
¼	cup tamari or soy sauce
1	knob fresh ginger root
4	tablespoons honey

black pepper to taste

Preparation is the key to wok cooking. Make sure all of the ingredients are ready to go so when you start stir-frying your timing is quick.

Cut the tofu into cubes. Cut the broccoli so the florets are intact. Slice the shiitake without the stems. Seed the bell pepper and cut it into strips. Peel and cut the carrot into diagonal slices. Chop the onion. Cut the bok choy diagonally including both the white and the green. Mince the garlic and crush the ginger.

Heat oil in a wok, bathing the sides and allowing it to be very hot. Add the onion and garlic, immediately followed by the tofu. Remember to drain and pat dry the tofu before throwing it in as wet tofu can splatter. Allow the tofu to brown.

Now add the vegetables. Vegetables should not be overcooked. They must be seared yet remain crisp, holding their chi (life force) which in turn gives the most nutritional value. Add the mushrooms first for they are best wilted and will absorb flavors. Add the broccoli and carrots next for they can stand more heat. Then toss in the red bell pepper followed by the soy sauce, ginger, honey and black pepper. Don't forget to stir constantly. Now add the most delicate vegetables; the bok choy and bean sprouts. Immediately turn off the heat. Remove from the wok and serve over rice.

Ma-shee-so!

Blue Lake Basin

FRIED BANANA DELIGHT

SERVES 2 TO 4

TEMPURA BATTER:

5	tablespoons flour
5	tablespoons cornstarch
⅔	cup water

THE REST:

1	banana
1	kiwi
½	mango
strawberries	
crushed peanuts	
Hershey's syrup	
vanilla ice cream	
oil for frying	

Combine the flour, corn starch and water and mix to a smooth consistency.

Cut the banana lengthwise and dip in the batter. Immerse in hot oil until golden brown. Drain excess oil on a paper towel. Put the banana on a plate and top with two scoops of ice cream. Garnish with fruit, chocolate sauce and peanuts.

Your tummy will be most happy!

made with joy in

JODY'S
KITCHEN
TELLURIDE, CO

Owner: Jody Borzilleri
728-6987

JOY CATERING

The inception of Joy Catering is an example of every dark cloud truly having a silver lining. "Joy started with a broken ankle," recalls owner Jody Borzilleri. "I was sitting on the porch wondering just what I was going to do to earn a living. A friend was building a house, so I made some goodies and took them over. You could say it all went from there."

Borzilleri named her company Joy because "I always used to tell the guys at the construction sites that I was delivering them joy, in the form of food." Indeed, the idea of delicious homemade goodies delivered via Jody's now famous bicycle and cart would incite joy in the recesses of any empty stomach.

Borzilleri has been towing her energy efficient, food-filled wagon around Telluride for the past three years. A native of Lake Placid, New York, she arrived, like many Telluridians, with the clear, unobstructed goal of skiing. After spending time at other Colorado ski resorts, she made her way south to Telluride with just $75 in her pocket. That was ten years ago. Now, Borzilleri enjoys the success nurtured by her entrepreneurial mind and her skiing (she finished second at the Shred-I Master in 1995, a three-day competition determining the best all-around snow athlete in the U.S., with competition in alpine and telemark skiing and snowboarding in moguls, gates and extreme).

In Telluride, her fame is mostly derived from her Chocolate Chip Congo Bars, the mere mention of which will make any locals' mouth water like a Pavlovian Dog's. Although Borzilleri will not divulge the recipe for her bars, let's just say they are sinfully wonderful and are worth the calorie-induced guilt (Congo Bars are offered in several Telluride eateries). In addition to Congo Bars, Borzilleri fills her energy-efficient cart with pumpkin bars, lemon squares, breakfast burritos, bagel sandwiches and roll-ups, which are a second cousin of the calzone.

HONEY WHOLE WHEAT BAGELS

MAKES 18 BAGELS

2½	cups hot water
¼	cup honey
2	tablespoons yeast
6	cups unbleached white flour
1	egg
2	teaspoons salt
3	cups whole wheat flour

In a large bowl, dissolve the honey in warm water. Slowly pour the yeast into the mixture while stirring. Let sit.

Add the six cups of white flour once the yeast begins to rise in the bowl. Stir until smooth and shiny. Allow to rise for 10 minutes.

Add the egg, salt and whole wheat flour and stir until you can't anymore. Knead for 5 minutes. Cover and let rest for 10 minutes. Shape into bagels starting with 3" balls. Bring water and 2 teaspoons of salt to a boil and add bagels. Boil for 20-30 seconds on both sides. Remove and bake at 350° for 20 minutes.

CRANBERRY ORANGE BREAD

4	eggs
4	tablespoons butter, melted
2	cups milk
6	cups flour
2	teaspoons salt
2	teaspoons baking powder
1	cup sugar

grated rind of one orange

2   cups cranberries, chopped in a food processor

Blend the eggs, melted butter and milk.

In a separate bowl, mix the flour, salt, baking powder and ½ cup of sugar. Next, mix the egg mixture and the flour mixture together.

In a third bowl, mix the cranberries, grated orange rind and the remaining ½ cup of sugar. Fold into the batter.

Pour into 2 greased bread pans and bake at 350° for 45 minutes or until a knife comes out clean.

Best to let stand for a couple of hours before slicing.

High Altitude Recipe: Refer to page 12

PUMPKIN PIE BARS

16	oz. canned pumpkin
½	cup vegetable oil
4	eggs
2	cups flour
¾	cup sugar
¾	cup brown sugar
1½	teaspoons baking powder
½	teaspoon baking soda
1	teaspoon salt
12	tablespoons margarine
1	teaspoon allspice
1	cup chocolate chips (optional)

Mix the pumpkin, oil and eggs. Add the rest of the ingredients, except the allspice, and mix. Add the allspice and, if you desire, the chocolate chips. Pour into a greased 10" x 13" glass baking dish and bake at 325° for 25 minutes.

Ed Note: *A cup of raisins also makes an excellent mix-in for this recipe and complements the pumpkin perfectly.*

High Altitude Recipe: Refer to page 12

MMM MMM MINT FUDGE

3	cups chocolate chips
4	tablespoons butter
14	oz. can sweetened condensed milk
1½	tablespoons peppermint extract
1½	teaspoons vanilla extract
dash of salt	
2	cups mini marshmallows

Melt the chocolate chips over low heat.

Add 2 tablespoons of butter, the condensed milk, peppermint, vanilla and salt. Mix over low heat until combined and spread in a 8"-9" square pan lined with aluminum foil.

In a separate pan, melt the marshmallows with the remaining 2 tablespoons of butter. Spoon onto the fudge and swirl through with a metal spatula or table knife.

Refrigerate for 2 hours or until firm.

Eat, smile!

CREATIVE FOODS

Owner: Kendra Wilcox
728-7222

KENDRA'S KITCHEN CREATIVE FOODS

Caterer Kendra Wilcox, owner of Kendra's Kitchen Creative Foods, has always been something of an entrepreneur. In high school, while her classmates were pondering the day's outfit, Wilcox was running her own pizza business. A physician's daughter who has traveled all over the world, Wilcox grew up eating gourmet and organic foods. Of her culinary childhood, she says, "We didn't eat hot dogs, we ate salmon!"

The personal chef of designer Ralph Lauren for four and a half years, Wilcox started Kendra's Kitchen in 1987, specializing in Southwestern cuisine and her own line of bottled seasonings.

Innovation in food design and preparation is Wilcox's trademark. She views cooking the way an artist might view painting. This attention to detail is evident in her catering style. Color is one of her great loves and she uses it to bring surprise to her creations. Two of her more popular dishes are quail with cranberry sauce, and a grilled yellow summer squash quesadilla.

When Wilcox isn't cooking, she's riding horses or traveling (Provence, South America, Asia, Europe, North Africa), searching for new ways to prepare and present food. "I'm always trying to develop my creative imagination," she says. "I get a lot of satisfaction from working hard, but I'm not a workaholic. I know how important it is to find a balance in your life, whether it's with food or your career."

VEGETABLE QUESADILLAS

SERVES 9 TO 12

12	6" flour tortillas
3	zucchini, sliced 1/16" thick, lengthwise
3	yellow squash, sliced 1/16" thick, lengthwise
½	Bermuda onion, slice in 1/16" rounds
1	red bell pepper, seeded and sliced in 1/16" rounds
½	cup grated mozzarella cheese
1	cup grated Monterey Jack cheese
¼	cup top quality grated Parmesan cheese

GRILL MARINADE:

½	cup apple jelly
¼	cup water
2	tablespoons Chimayo chile powder
2	teaspoons ground cumin
1-2	teaspoons crushed red pepper flakes

Mix the marinade ingredients. Coat the vegetables with it and let stand while preparing the rest of the recipe.

Mix the cheeses and set aside.

Grill the vegetables until cooked. Set aside.

Melt a little butter or olive oil in a skillet. Place a flour tortilla in the skillet. Sprinkle with cheese and grilled vegetables. Top with another flour tortilla. When the first side is browned, flip and brown the other side. Repeat with the rest of the tortillas and filling.

You may grill the quesadillas, eliminating the butter and giving you a larger cooking space.

Serve with your favorite salsa, guacamole and creme fraiche or sour cream.

Ed. Note: *This marinade could be used with great success for any grilling, particularly steaks and chicken, giving them a sweet and spicy Southwestern flavor.*

FILLET OF BEEF OR ELK STEAKS WITH A PASILLA SAUCE

SERVES 4

2	Pasilla chiles
1	Anaheim chile
7	ripe plum tomatoes
½	large white onion, coarsely chopped
3	garlic cloves
1	tablespoon olive oil
1	cup chicken stock
2	tablespoons cilantro
4	6 oz. beef or elk fillets

Heat a skillet, add the chiles and toast for five minutes. Cool and remove the stems and seeds. Cut into large pieces.

Place the tomatoes, onion and garlic in frying pan. Cook on high for 2-3 minutes. Add one tablespoon olive oil and continue cooking for another 5 minutes. Add the chicken stock and mix.

Place the sauce and chopped chiles in a food processor or blender and blend until smooth. Strain the sauce if you prefer a smooth consistency.

Sear the steaks in a frying pan over medium-high heat to desired temperature. Remove the steaks, but reserve the cooking juices.

Add the pureed sauce to the meat juices in the pan. Taste for seasoning. Add Southwestern seasoning from Kendra's Kitchen* or salt, pepper and a little brown sugar to taste. Simmer for 15 minutes, adding water if the sauce becomes too thick. Add 2 tablespoons chopped cilantro. Serve the steaks with the sauce and top with avocado relish (see page 80).

*Kendra's Seasoning is available at Telluride retail stores, or through the Internet: http://www.kendras_kitchen.com.

AVOCADO RELISH:

2	ripe avocados, peeled and diced
½	red bell pepper, seeded and diced
½	Bermuda onion, diced
1	tablespoon fresh cilantro

juice of ¼ lime

½	teaspoon salt

Mix all of the ingredients together and let sit, covered, until ready to serve.

Telluride's Annual Balloon Festival

LOW-FAT CHOCOLATE CUSTARD CAKE

1	cup all-purpose flour
¾	cup sugar
2	tablespoons unsweetened cocoa
1	tablespoon instant coffee
1½	teaspoons baking powder
¼	teaspoon salt
½	cup 1% low-fat milk
⅓	cup oil
1	teaspoon vanilla extract
1	cup firmly packed brown sugar
¼	cup unsweetened cocoa
1¾	cups boiling water

Combine the first 6 ingredients in a 9" square baking pan and stir well. Add the milk, oil and vanilla and stir until smooth. In a separate bowl, combine the brown sugar and ¼ cup cocoa and sprinkle over the batter. Pour the boiling water over the batter, but do not stir. Bake at 375° for 45-50 minutes. Serve warm with the fresh raspberries and raspberry sauce.

Ed. Note: *An amazingly rich cake for such a small amount of rich ingredients.*

❖ LA MARMOTTE ❖
RESTAURANT FRANÇAIS

Owners: Bertrand & Noelle Lepel-Cointet
Chef: Bertrand Marchal
150 West San Juan Avenue
728-6232

LA MARMOTTE

Named for the marmot, a gregarious, furry brown critter that lives in mountain burrows and hibernates in the winter, La Marmotte, is one of Telluride's most prized culinary possessions. Housed in the historic brick Ice House, this lyrically named French restaurant has won accolades for its sumptuous entrees and desserts. Chef and part-owner Bertrand Marchal worked in the French Alps and Canada, and spent eight years in other U.S. locales before moving to Telluride five years ago.

His cuisine, which he describes as "not too fancy but really good and tasty," includes imaginative plays on the traditional onion soup, creme brulee, rack of lamb and other French favorites. Using fresh thyme and rosemary, Marchal layers flavors into his food much like a painter layers colors on a canvas. The results are obviously pleasing to the restaurant's legion of loyal patrons, some of whom call weeks in advance for a table.

Of his talent, Marchal says simply, "A lot of it is improvisation and intuition. You just know when some things are going to be good together." La Marmotte's team seems good together indeed. Husband-and-wife co-owners Bertrand and Noelle Lepel-Cointet purposely avoided what Noelle calls a "nose up" tack, opting instead to keep the food and the decor simple and unpretentious. And Chef Marchal emphasizes that just because the food is French doesn't mean it is butter and cream laden. He follows a healthier approach, nonetheless still reminding diners that "Taste should be more important than fat content." Well said. This subtle French restaurant is a treat during any season and only hibernates in the off-season.

VEAL SWEETBREADS WITH CALVADOS SAUCE & ALSATIAN SAUERKRAUT

SERVES 4

1	pound sauerkraut
4	slices bacon
½	onion, chopped
1	bay leaf, whole
a couple of juniper berries	
1½	pounds veal sweetbreads
2	apples
¼	cup sugar
1	cup veal stock
3	oz. Calvados
2	shallots, chopped
1	cup white wine

Rinse the sauerkraut under warm water and squeeze out the water.

In a sauce pot, saute the onion with the bacon. Add the sauerkraut, wine, a bay leaf and a couple of juniper berries. Cook for an hour at very low heat.

In a separate pot, bring the sweetbreads to boil in water with a little vinegar and salt. Let them boil for two minutes.

Peel and cut the apples into large cubes. Saute in butter and ¼ cup of sugar until they caramelize.

Saute the sweetbreads in butter until they are golden on both sides. Add the shallots and then deglaze with the Calvados. Add the veal stock and reduce the sauce by half. Add the caramelized apples and season with salt and pepper.

Slice the sweetbreads and serve atop the sauerkraut. The sweetness of the Calvados sauce and the tartness of the sauerkraut are an excellent combination.

Serve with an Alsatian white wine such as a Pinot Gris or a Riesling.

SAUTEED SEA SCALLOPS IN A CARROT & DRY VERMOUTH SAUCE WITH FRENCH GREEN BEANS & BASMATI RICE

SERVES 6

2½	pounds fresh large sea scallops
1	pound carrots, sliced
1	small onion, chopped
1	cup dry Vermouth
3	cups fish stock
1	pound fresh baby green beans (haricots verts)

cooked basmati rice for 6
lemon juice

THE CARROT SAUCE:

In a sauce pot, saute the onion and carrots in a little bit of olive oil until they start to color. Deglaze with the Vermouth and add the fish stock. Cook for about 10 minutes.

Put the sauce in a blender or food processor and process until smooth. Season with salt, pepper and a little bit of lemon juice. Keep warm.

THE SCALLOPS:

Cook the beans in salted boiling water until tender. Plunge in ice cold water so they stop cooking and retain their green color.

Salt and pepper the scallops. Heat some butter or margarine in a non-stick frying pan. Add the scallops and cook for a few minutes on both sides until they have a nice brown color.

Heat the green beans in a pan with some butter.

To serve, put the carrot sauce in the button of a plate and add rice in the middle. Arrange the beans around the rice and add the scallops.

GLAZED FRESH BERRY SABAYON

SERVES 4

4   eggs
3   egg yolks
⅔   cup sugar
1   cup heavy cream, whipped
a few drops of vanilla extract
1   teaspoon grated fresh ginger
1   pint mixed berries (raspberries, strawberries, blackberries...)

In a mixer bowl, combine the eggs and yolks and whip over low heat until foamy and warm.

At the same time, boil the sugar with 1 cup of water to make a syrup.

Put the bowl with the eggs back on the mixer and whip on high speed. Pour the boiling syrup into the eggs and continue to whip until the sabayon is cool. Add the vanilla, ginger and whipped cream.

Put the berries in a bowl and cover with the sabayon. Glaze under a hot broiler for a few seconds. Add a scoop of your favorite ice cream.

Sam Bush performs at the Telluride Bluegrass Festival

LEGENDS
OF THE PEAKS

Located in The Peaks At Telluride Resort
136 Country Club Drive
Mountain Village
728-6800

LEGENDS OF THE PEAKS

The menu at Legends Of The Peaks has been designed to pay homage to the unsung heroes of Telluride's past. The back of the menu notes: "Would mining have prospered in the rugged and remote Telluride Valley had it not been for the mule? Probably not." There are other true legends of course: the Native Americans, the miners toiling at 11,000 feet for dollars a day and the 'Ladies of the Evening' working in the cribs of the Red Light District on East Pacific Avenue.

Legends' menu is not only an interesting history lesson. Inside, it features selections as dazzling as the mountain views framed by the restaurant's picture windows. Executive Chef Robert Kowalske works on two main themes: hearty Ranchlands Cuisine and low-fat Peaks Performance Cuisine.

The Ranchlands Menu includes herb crusted range chicken with grilled citrus vinaigrette and roasted vegetable hash; barbecued ahi steak with black beans, roasted corn and braised greens; and apple wood smoked tenderloin of beef served with grilled vegetables, red onion confit and crisp potato wedges.

Peaks Performance Cuisine offers linguini primavera with basil and Parmigiano-Reggiano; char-broiled shrimp with Asian noodles, bok choy, snow peas and a blend of oriental flavors; and handcrafted pizza of cilantro pesto, yellow tomato, shaved fennel, red onion and low-fat Feta cheese on a cornmeal crust.

Kowalske uses locally-grown produce whenever possible. Freshness is key and through roasting, smoking and grilling, he gently coaxes each food's flavor to its zenith, enhancing it with fresh rosemary, basil and thyme, his herbs of choice.

"What we do here is take common foods and prepare them in uncommon ways," Kowalske says. "We claim to have the most spectacular views of any restaurant in Telluride and we have the food to match."

ROASTED GARLIC, POTATO & CORN CHOWDER

SERVES 6

2	garlic bulbs
6	medium ears of corn
6	strips turkey bacon, cut into ½ inch pieces
1	small onion, finely chopped
1	small green pepper, finely chopped
1	jalapeno pepper, seeded, deveined and finely chopped
1	small celery stalk, finely chopped
1	tomato, peeled, seeded and cubed
2	medium boiled red potatoes, cubed
1	teaspoon salt

a pinch of sugar

1	small bay leaf
3	cups chicken stock
½	cup half and half

freshly ground black pepper

chopped parsley for garnish

Cut off the top ½ inch of both garlic bulbs and place in a small baking pan. Drizzle olive oil over the tops of the bulbs and cover the pan with foil. Place in a 250° oven for 90 minutes, or until the garlic is golden brown and soft when probed with a fork. Let cool and then squeeze the cloves of garlic out of the cut ends and reserve.

Working over a bowl, cut the corn kernels from the cobs at about half their depth. Using the back of a knife, scrape the cobs over the bowl to release all the milk. Set aside.

In a large saucepan, cook the bacon over moderately high heat, flipping occasionally, until crisp; about 10 minutes. Transfer the bacon to paper towels to drain, reserving the drippings in the pan. Set aside.

Discard all but 3 tablespoons of the bacon drippings from the pan. Add the onion and cook over moderate heat until golden; 4 to 5 minutes. Add the bell pepper, jalapeno pepper and celery and cook until slightly softened; about 2 minutes. Add the tomatoes, potatoes, salt, sugar, bay leaf, roasted garlic and reserved corn kernels with their milk and stir well. Cook over moderate heat until the mixture begins to sizzle.

Reduce heat to low. Cover and cook, stirring occasionally until the potatoes are tender; 35 to 40 minutes. Stir in the chicken stock and half & half and bring to a boil. Remove from heat and season with black pepper and more salt to taste. Ladle the chowder into bowls and garnish with parsley and the reserved bacon.

Nordic racing in the Mountain Village

GRILLED VEGETABLE CASSEROLE

SERVES 4

1	large zucchini, sliced thin and grilled
1	large yellow squash, sliced thin and grilled
12	oz. quinoa, cooked according to package directions
2	medium red onions, julienned and caramelized
6	medium red potatoes, sliced in ¼" rounds and blanched
1	bunch spinach, cleaned
1	medium butternut squash, peeled and thinly sliced
4	medium red peppers, roasted, seeded and peeled
20	medium shiitake mushroom caps, grilled
1	tablespoon chopped garlic
1	tablespoon chopped fresh oregano and thyme
4	individual ceramic casserole dishes

parchment paper
non-stick vegetable spray
salt and pepper to taste

Cut out circles of parchment paper to fit the bottom of each casserole dish. Generously spray the bottom and inner sides of each dish with non-stock spray. Lay parchment into the bottoms of the dishes and spray again.

Lay new potatoes into the bottom overlapping each other to form a spiral. As you go, sprinkle each layer with a little salt and pepper. Next, layer the yellow squash. Then add a layer of spinach, the caramelized onion, garlic, herbs and the mushrooms.

Take about ¼ of the quinoa and spread an even layer across the mushrooms. Layer next with zucchini, then butternut squash and the whole red pepper last.

Place the casserole dishes on a pan, cover with foil and bake at 325° for 60 minutes.

ROASTED GARLIC MASHED POTATOES

SERVES 4 TO 6

2	pounds red potatoes, cut into large dice
1	cup of warmed half & half
4	tablespoons softened butter
4	garlic bulbs
1	teaspoon black pepper
1	tablespoon olive oil

Cut off the top ½ inch of each garlic bulb and place in a small baking pan. Drizzle olive oil over the tops of the bulbs and cover the pan with foil. Place in a 250° oven for 90 minutes, or until the garlic is golden brown and soft when probed with a fork. Let cool.

In a large pot with salted boiling water (about 2 tablespoons per gallon), add the potatoes and simmer for 20 minutes or until tender. Strain the potatoes and place in a large mixing bowl. With beaters or a wire whisk, slowly whip until smooth.

Add the softened butter and warm half & half and mix until fully incorporated. Squeeze the cloves of garlic out of the cut end. Mash the garlic in a small bowl with a fork and add it to the potatoes. Finish with salt and pepper to taste. Enjoy!

LOW-FAT COOKIES

MAKES 18 TO 24 COOKIES

1¾	cups unbleached white flour
½	cup whole wheat flour
½	teaspoon baking soda
8	tablespoons margarine
⅓	cup brown sugar
1	tablespoon vanilla
1	egg
2	egg whites
½	cup apple juice
½	teaspoon cinnamon
⅛	teaspoon ground clove
¼	teaspoon nutmeg
¼	cup raisins
¼	cup currants
1	teaspoon orange zest

Sift together the dry ingredients.

In a mixing bowl, cream the margarine and sugar together. Add the vanilla.

Mix the whole egg with the egg whites and mix into the margarine and sugar. Stir in the apple juice, dry ingredients and spices. Stir in the raisins, currants and orange zest.

Drop spoonfuls of dough onto a cookie sheet and bake at 350° for 10-12 minutes.

Ed. Note: *This is not a sweet cookie, but more like a great scone.*

Cracked Canyon climbing - Ophir

Owner: Christel Leimgruber
573 West Pacific Street
728-4663

LEIMGRUBER'S BIERSTUBE & RESTAURANT

Leimgruber's Bierstube and Restaurant is synonymous with apres-ski in Telluride. On any winter's afternoon, the restaurant's deck teems with high-on-life skiers clunking around in ski boots and bibs long after the lifts have stopped running.

Owner Christel Leimgruber opened her Bavarian restaurant in the winter of 1986, taking her goal of German authenticity to the smallest detail. Her waitresses wear traditional dirndls fashioned in Leimgruber's home town of Prien am Chiemsee, a small Bavarian hamlet close to Munich and Salzburg, Austria, in Germany's alpine region.

The restaurant's motto is Gemutlichkeit, a German term meaning "to feel comfortable." Comfort, it seems, dictates the layout of Leimgruber's. The atmosphere is casual, the air clean (Leimgruber's was Telluride's first non-smoking restaurant and bar). While waiting for your meal you can learn something new as the menu lists 25 interesting facts about Bavaria, such as a mention that the Bavarian Alps boast Germany's highest mountain: the 9,724-foot Zugspitze, from the summit of which Italy is visible.

Housed in a miner's cabin built in 1913, the bierstube serves Paulaner beers (hailed as Munich's number #1 beer) and features a menu of traditional Bavarian food, including rouladen (sirloin beef tips seasoned and stuffed with onions, pickles and bacon); the Leimgruber Hausplatte (smoked pork chops served with red and white cabbage and parsley potatoes); a wild game sausage plate; wienerschnitzel; apple strudel; and Black Forest cheesecake. For those not in the mood for German food, the menu also offers pasta, chicken, smoked trout, and a variety of soups and desserts, which Leimgruber makes herself.

With its two decks, one in front and one in back, Leimgruber's is an inviting place to spend any sunny afternoon. Regardless of the time of year, visitors to this cozy historic house will remember it for its distinctive German feel and hospitality. Guten Appetit!

CHRISTEL'S BAKED BRIE WITH APPLE-LINGONBERRY SAUCE

SERVES 4

1	wedge brie
¼	cup walnut pieces
½	apple, sliced
1	tablespoon apple-lingonberry sauce

bread slices

Place the brie on an oven-proof plate. Put it in a 400° oven for 10 minutes or until the cheese begins to melt slightly.

To make the apple-lingonberry sauce, combine the apple slices with the lingonberries, which you can find in the grocery store's jam and jelly aisle. Serve the brie with bread and the sauce on the side.

LEIMGRUBER'S WIENERSCHNITZEL

16   oz. veal tenderloin, pounded
1   cup plain breadcrumbs
4   eggs, beaten with 4 tablespoons of water
salt and pepper to taste
½   cup clarified butter (does not blacken when heated)

Salt and pepper both sides of the veal. Dip the veal in the egg mixture and coat with the bread crumbs. Clarify the butter by heating it and skimming the foam off the top. Heat the clarified butter over high heat, place the veal in the pan and quickly brown both sides.

Garnish each plate with a lemon wedge, capers and anchovies. Serve with boiled potatoes and red cabbage.

CHRISTEL'S APPLE STRUDEL

SERVES 4 TO 6

THE FILLING:

⅓   cup rum-soaked raisins
juice of 1 lemon
½   cup ground walnuts
½   teaspoon cinnamon
4   medium cooking apples
⅔   cup of sugar
6   tablespoons sour cream
¼   teaspoon ground cloves

Soak the raisins in rum for 2-3 hours. Peel and finely slice the apples. Sprinkle the apples with the lemon juice. In a small bowl, combine the raisins, sugar, nuts, sour cream and spices. Add the apple slices and carefully toss to distribute.

THE STRUDEL:

1   pound frozen filo dough
8   tablespoons melted butter
plain bread crumbs

Thaw the filo in a container overnight. Place a clean towel or cheesecloth on a flat surface. Place 1 sheet of filo on a towel and brush with butter. Place another sheet on top and brush with butter. Repeat with 4 more sheets. Butter the last sheet and sprinkle with plain bread crumbs. Spread ⅓ of the filling on the edge of the dough and shape like a loaf.

Roll the filo using the towel to help lift it. Pinch the edges to seal. Grab the towel on each side of the loaf, lift and place the loaf on a greased baking sheet. Carefully remove the towel. Repeat with the remaining filo, making three strudels.

Brush the tops with beaten butter and egg and sprinkle with cinnamon and brown sugar. Bake at 400° until golden brown.

Serve warm with whipped cream and a scoop of ice cream.

Bridal Veil Falls - Colorado's highest free-falling waterfall

Owner: Lito Nepomiachi
300 South Mahoney Drive
(at the base of the Coonskin Lift)
728-0770

LITO'S CAFE & TAPAS BAR

What exactly are 'tapas'? According to Lito Nepomiachi, owner of Lito's Cafe, the explanation is found in the dubious tactics of a Spanish barkeeper named Don Julio Dominquez, who found a rather ingenious way to increase profits at his Andalucian bar. When a customer ordered a drink, the barman would place a salty morsel of food atop the glass. The customer would eat the thirst-inducing tidbit and, naturally, order another drink, over which would sit another portion of salty food.

The ingenious dishes were dubbed 'tapas' from the Spanish verb tapir, meaning 'to cover.' The idea of the appetizer grew in popularity and is now a Spanish custom in which people gather for cold drinks and tapas. Here in Telluride, Lito's Cafe and Bar carries on the tradition.

A native of Buenos Aires, Argentina, Nepomiachi moved to Telluride in August 1994 and opened his restaurant that December. "I owned a bar in the Chicago area for 12 years, sold it and went to Florida with the intention of opening a restaurant," he says. "Not too long after arriving in Florida, I said to myself, 'Forget about the ocean, let's go to the mountains.'" An accomplished chef, Nepomiachi began cooking at the age of 16. Extensively trained in the restaurants of Spain, Nepomiachi specializes in the Mediterranean cuisine of Greece, Italy and Spain.

Located at the base of the Coonskin chair lift, Lito's glass enclosed dining room and bar are favorites with skiers eating lunch and the apres ski crowd. The cafe is also well-known for its one-of-a-kind bar, a smooth slab of cement resting atop wood harvested from an old Telluride mine. The foot rail is also unique: no fan of the ordinary, Nepomiachi installed an old train rail, once used by the Rio Grande Southern Railroad, on which patrons can now rest their ski-weary feet.

WHITE ASPARAGUS GAZPACHO

SERVES 4

1	pound white asparagus, peeled
2	quarts light chicken stock
juice of one orange	
3	oz. stale bread crumbs
1	clove garlic
3	tablespoons olive oil
1	teaspoon sherry vinegar

Cut the top 1½ inches of the tips of the asparagus from the stalks. Slice the tips thinly and cook in boiling water for 2 minutes. Drain and rinse in cold water.

Cut the asparagus stalks into chunks and put in a pot with chicken stock and orange juice. Cook until very tender; about 40 minutes. Add the bread to the liquid and let soak.

Spoon out the asparagus and bread and mix in a blender with the garlic. Add the olive oil and vinegar. Stir the puree back into the remaining broth, add salt to taste and chill.

Ladle into soup bowls garnished with minced green onion.

LEMON PASTA WITH VEGGIE MIX

SERVES 4

1	tablespoon vegetable oil
zest of ½ lemon	
¼	red bell pepper, seeded and cut into thin strips
1	green onion, cut into rings
¼	small white onion, cut into thin rings
⅛	small fennel bulb, cut into thin strips
½	cup thinly sliced cabbage
1	pound linguini, cooked al dente

Heat the oil with the lemon zest in a large skillet over medium-high heat. Add the red pepper, fennel bulb and green and white onion. Stir-fry for 2-3 minutes until the vegetables begin to soften. Add the cabbage and cook for 1 more minute until the cabbage is wilted. Add the pasta and warm to desired temperature. Salt to taste and serve.

COCONUT-CARAMEL FLAN

Flan, of Spanish origin, is the standard dessert of all Latin America. The coconut adds a unique taste.

SERVES 12

THE CARAMEL:

1	cup sugar
1½	tablespoons water
3-5	drops fresh lemon juice

Put the sugar, water and lemon juice in a small sauce pan. Over low heat, stir to dissolve the sugar.

When the mixture comes to a boil, raise the heat to medium and, without stirring, let the sugar syrup cook for 8 to 10 minutes until brown.

Quickly pour the syrup into an ungreased 8 cup mold, swirling it so that the caramel covers the bottom and sides. Let cool.

THE CUSTARD:

4½	cups milk
4	eggs
8	egg yolks
1	cup sugar
1	vanilla bean
1	tablespoon raw, unsweetened coconut (or more to taste)

Preheat oven to 350°. Put the coconut on a baking sheet and toast for 10 to 12 minutes, stirring often, until golden. Let cool.

Bring the milk to a boil with the vanilla bean, then remove the vanilla bean. In a mixing bowl, beat the eggs, yolks and sugar, stirring constantly. Add the hot milk to the egg mixture. Add the coconut and pour into the caramelized mold.

Set the mold into a deep pan slightly larger than it. Fill the pan with boiling water that reaches halfway up the side of the mold. Bake for approximately 60 minutes at 325°.

Separate the custard from the mold and turn onto a platter deep enough to hold the caramel liquid. Let cool before serving.

Just another day at the office for Roudy Roudebush

Ms. Cheesecake Too!!

Owner: Sally Wilkinson
728-5613

MS. CHEESECAKE TOO!!

With a name like Ms. Cheesecake Too!!, caterer Sally Wilkinson certainly has no trouble getting people's attention. But behind the quirky name is extraordinary food presented in innovative ways and always with a touch of Wilkinson flair.

Before discovering Telluride, Wilkinson owned Houston's popular Ms. Cheesecake Etc., which offered a full restaurant menu and catering service and featured her wildly popular Killer Double Chocolate Chip Cheesecake. In Telluride, Wilkinson is known for her wedding cakes and specialized wedding catering.

Not content to confine her talents to the traditional white wedding cake, she creates unique confections with interesting twists: chocolate cake laced with Chambord (raspberry liqueur), filled with raspberries and covered with white buttercream; spicy carrot cake with pecans and pineapple; and Genoise with liqueur flavorings and fruit filling.

Beyond weddings, Wilkinson can cater just about any event and does so with a style that has become her trademark. One of her more popular menu items is Raspberry Chicken Breast, chicken poached in Champagne, glazed with a raspberry sauce and topped with fresh raspberries. The Champagne adds zing and the raspberries color, two important elements in Wilkinson's cooking.

Wilkinson, who earned A's in chemistry and physics, has become a master of high-altitude baking. She offers these tips to keep baking attempts at high altitude from falling flat: decrease sugar one tablespoon per cup, increase flour two tablespoons per cup and decrease leavening (baking powder or soda) by a quarter teaspoon per teaspoon.

She suggests, "Don't overfill your pans. Lots of recipes are ruined by overmixing, which creates excess air in the batter and causes the cake to over-rise and collapse. Trust me on this. When I first moved here, I made many hungry birds very happy!"

2 DIPS: PICCADILLY MEXICANO & GREEN CHILE

SERVES 12

PICCADILLY MEXICANO:

"I vary this recipe according to whatever amounts of ingredients I have on hand. It really doesn't seem to make a lot of difference, except the amount of chutney should remain constant."

2	pounds ground hamburger or ground round
1	hot sausage (Italian sausage is good and lean)
1	medium onion, diced
2	teaspoons minced garlic
3	large tomatoes, chopped and seeded (canned will do)
½	4 oz. can diced jalapeno peppers (careful: this is just to taste)
1	cup sliced almonds
1½	cups raisins
1	teaspoon oregano (fresh is better)
½	bottle mango chutney (fresh mangos in season may be substituted)

Saute the meats and drain any grease. Add the onion and garlic and cook for 5 more minutes. Add the rest of the ingredients and heat through. If the mixture is too crumbly for a dip, add a little cornstarch liquid to thicken it.

GREEN CHILE DIPPING SAUCE:

1   packet ranch dressing mix
sour cream according to dressing package directions
a couple dashes of Tabasco
canned green chiles

Prepare the dressing according to the package directions. Add Tabasco and green chiles to taste. The dip may be thinned for dipping with butter-milk or milk. Serve both dips with a variety of blue, white and red corn chips.

GRILLED SALSA BLACKENED CHICKEN BREASTS

SERVES 4

2   cups salsa (a blend of mild and hot to your taste)
½   cup brown sugar
2   tablespoons Dijon or stone ground brown mustard
jalapenos and fresh cilantro to taste
4   skinned and deboned chicken breasts

Process salsa to a medium texture in a blender or food processor. Stir in the remaining ingredients, except the chicken.

The night before serving, place the chicken in a dish and baste with the salsa marinade. Turn the chicken in the morning and add more marinade.

Grill the chicken until done, turning once; about 20 minutes. Serve with extra marinade.

DILLED POTATO SALAD

SERVES 4 TO 6

2   pounds red potatoes
4   slices bacon
2   teaspoons dill
3-4   hard boiled eggs, chopped
8-10   slices bacon, baked and diced
To your taste:
        mayonnaise
        black olives, sliced
        sweet pickle relish
        dill pickle relish
cherry tomatoes for garnish

Dice potatoes to size for the salad. Place in a pot with raw bacon and dill. Cover with water and boil until just tender. Drain and remove potatoes and place in a serving bowl.

Mix in the eggs, baked bacon and the "ingredients to taste."

Chill before serving. Garnish with cherry tomatoes.

A powdery commute back to town...

A TRIFLE IN A CHOCOLATE TACO

This takes a little time to prepare, but is well worth the effort.

SERVES 12

CHOCOLATE TACO:

1	package taco shells
12	oz. chocolate chips

Use hard taco shells for the form. Cover outside of a shell with aluminum foil. Melt chocolate chips in the microwave or in a pan over hot water. Using a paint brush or pastry brush, 'paint' chocolate over aluminum foil. Refrigerate each taco. When chocolate is hard, apply a second coat in the same manner. When second coat is hard, carefully break taco loose from the form and peel off the foil. You will want to make extra shells to account for any breakage. Cover shells and place in freezer until ready to use.

CUSTARD:

8	cups milk
2	sticks butter
2⅓	cups sugar
2	teaspoons vanilla
12	egg yolks
5½	oz. cornstarch

fresh blueberries and raspberries or strawberries

Heat milk, butter, sugar and vanilla in a heavy sauce pan almost to the scald stage. Place egg yolks in a bowl. Put cornstarch in another bowl.

Whisk a little of the hot milk mixture into the cornstarch until smooth. [See note.] Whisk cornstarch into egg yolks. Then whisk the egg yolk-cornstarch mixture into the hot milk in a slow, steady stream. Whisk until custard is thick. Remove from stove and cover with buttered parchment paper to prevent skin from forming. Let cool.

When custard is cool, divide into three bowls. Cut with whipping cream if it is too thick.

[Note: *If you use a stainless steel whip, use a stainless steel pot. Otherwise, use a teflon whip and an aluminum pot. If you use a stainless steel whip with an aluminum pot, your sauce will turn grey from the chemical reaction.*]

SAUCES:

1   box recipe white or angel food cake or two dozen lady fingers
12   oz. semi-sweet chocolate chips
Grand Marnier of Grand Torres
1   pint raspberries or strawberries

SAUCE 1:

Melt 12 oz. semi-sweet chocolate chips, or a combination of milk and semi-sweet chocolate, in a microwave or a pan over simmering water. Whisk chocolate into the first bowl of custard, adding vanilla if needed.

SAUCE 2:

Cover ½ pint of raspberries or strawberries with Grand Torres or Grand Marnier. Heat at a low temperature. When berries are soft, push through a fine sieve or cheesecloth so no seeds end up in the sauce. Whisk most of this mixture into the second bowl of custard, reserving a little.

SAUCE 3:

Leave custard 3 plain.

ASSEMBLING THE TACOS:

Place dessert plates in refrigerator to cool. Melt more chocolate chips and let cool. Spoon a strip of cooled chocolate down the middle of a dessert plate. Carefully place a chocolate taco shell in an upright position on the chocolate strip. Repeat with each plate. Place in freezer and let set.

Break cake into small pieces and place in a bowl. Drizzle the reserved fruit sauce over cake pieces until wet, but not soggy.

Remove taco shells from freezer and layer as follows: cake - chocolate custard - blueberries - cake - fruit custard - raspberries or strawberries.

Spoon plain custard sauce around the base of the taco shell and decorate with more fruit.

Serve at once!

THE NATURAL SOURCE

Owners: James & Ivy Rainwater
236 West Colorado Avenue
728-4833

THE NATURAL SOURCE

The Natural Source, Telluride's natural food store and deli, vigorously dispels the notion that vegetarian food cannot be gourmet. The Natural Source features an impressive selection of rich, incredibly flavorful vegan foods (vegan meaning food containing no animal products, not even milk or eggs). Says Ivy Rainwater, co-owner with husband James, "There are three elements to the vegan philosophy: eating for personal health, eating for planetary health and developing a sense of compassion for other forms of life."

The Rainwaters arrived in Telluride from the neighboring ski town of Crested Butte. They had spent years dreaming of owning a natural food store, but lacked the resources to bring the idea to fruition. After spending months on a business plan, a bank loan came through and they found themselves in Telluride. For James, it was a homecoming of sorts as he had lived in Telluride as a teenager.

The Natural Source is a natural food lover's dream. In addition to its selection of locally grown, organic produce and bulk grains, beans, mixes, spices and herbs, the store also sells vitamin and mineral supplements and herbal and homeopathic remedies. The most popular section is the vegan deli featuring such meatless delights as tempeh reubens and burgers, hummus sandwiches, stuffed grape leaves and an organic salad bar. The store also prepares vegan cakes and bakes and sells organic vegan muffins, cookies and breads. To truly experience the vegan sublime, try the coconut cream pie or a custom-made smoothie; Ivy guarantees you'll never miss the dairy.

Vegetarians and carnivores alike are welcomed to the store with open arms. "Everything in life is about making a choice," says Ivy. "If you decide to eat a vegan meal, then you are doing something positive for yourself and the Earth. We show people that vegan food can be gourmet and in the process gently encourage them to make the vegan choice again and again."

TEMPEH SLOPPY JOES

SERVES 4

2	8 oz. tempeh cakes
1	green pepper, diced
1	small onion, diced
1	teaspoon cumin powder
1	teaspoon garlic powder
2	teaspoons black pepper
1-2	teaspoons sea salt
2	tablespoons olive oil
1	15 oz. can tomato sauce

In oil, saute the onion and pepper for 5 minutes. Crumble in the tempeh and stir in the spices and sauce. Cook for 10 minutes. Serve hot on a bun.

BBQ TOFU & VEGETABLES

SERVES 4

THE BBQ SAUCE:

⅓	cup maple syrup
⅓	cup tamari soy sauce
2	tablespoons garlic powder
2	tablespoons apple cider vinegar
½	teaspoon sea salt
1	teaspoon cumin
1	teaspoon black pepper

In a bowl, mix all of the sauce ingredients.

THE SAUTE:

1	onion, diced
1	green pepper, diced
1	zucchini, diced
1	pound hard tofu, diced
2	tablespoons oil

Saute the vegetables and tofu in the oil until they begin to release their juices.

Mix in the BBQ sauce and cook for 10 minutes over low heat. Serve over rice.

STEAMED VEGETABLES
WITH SPICY PEANUT SAUCE

SERVES 4

PEANUT SAUCE:

1	small onion, minced
1	clove garlic, crushed
2	tablespoons olive oil
2	cups water
1⅓	cups peanut butter
1	tablespoon tamari soy sauce
1	teaspoon black pepper
1	teaspoon garlic powder
¼	teaspoon cayenne pepper
1	teaspoon sea salt (less if using salted peanut butter)

Saute the onion and garlic in the oil until soft. Add the water, peanut butter, tamari and spices. Whisk well while cooking over low heat until creamy.

Serve over steamed vegetables and couscous, rice or another grain.

I CAN'T BELIEVE IT'S VEGAN
TOFU MUD PIE

1	cup walnuts
1½	cups dairyless chocolate chips
1½	pounds soft tofu
⅓	cup chocolate soy milk
1	teaspoon vanilla extract
⅛-¼	cup maple syrup

Blend all of the ingredients in a food processor or blender for five minutes until fully pureed. Turn into a pie shell and bake at 350° for 30 minutes. Chill for one hour before serving.

Ed. Note: *Even people who are not tofu fans love this rich, chocolate mousse-like pie.*

PACIFIC STREET MARKET

And

Bread & Roses Catering

Owners: John & Janice Gerona
627 West Pacific Street
728-5246

PACIFIC STREET MARKET
AND BREAD & ROSES CATERING

Like many who relocate their lives and careers to Telluride, transplanted New Yorkers John and Janice Gerona arrived with a specific goal in mind: getting back to nature and onto the ski slopes.

John, from Queens, and Janice, from Long Island, moved here within a year of each other and were roommates before they married. Once hitched, Janice, who has a degree in restaurant management, and John, the former head chef at Telluride's French restaurant, La Marmotte, opened their first business together. Naturally, they opted to stay close to food and decided to start an upscale food market. Says Janice, "We fell in love and decided to feed the world."

Modeled after Zabar's, Manhattan's famous gourmet food store, Pacific Street Market opened in the summer of 1993, selling imported cheeses, meats and other specialty items as well as some of the most imaginative sandwiches in town. Sandwich favorites include falafel, turkey with cranberry sauce, and the Pacific Street Market Club. For lovers of real New York bagels, the Geronas have them flown in from H & H Bagels in Manhattan.

In addition to their market, the Geronas also own Bread and Roses Catering, offering custom-made wedding and birthday cakes and a wide selection of cheese trays, casseroles and special dinners for any occasion.

Says John, "We want people to know we conducted a good deal of research before opening our business. That included eating at lots of New York City delis, sometimes going back again and again to discover new combinations and flavors." Sounds like a tough job, doesn't it?

TABBOULEH SALAD

SERVES 6

1	cup bulgar wheat
⅝	cup finely chopped onion
⅜	cup chopped scallions
¾	teaspoon salt
¼	teaspoon ground black pepper
1¼	cups chopped Italian parsley
⅜	cup fresh mint, chopped
⅜	cup lemon juice
¼	cup extra virgin olive oil
¾	cup peeled tomatoes, chopped

Cover the bulgar wheat with water and let stand for 2 hours. Drain excess water. Add the rest of the ingredients, mix well and serve.

CURRIED CHICKEN SALAD

SERVES 8

3	cups cooked, chopped chicken
¾	cup chopped onion
1	cup chopped celery
½	cup seeded and chopped red bell pepper
1	cup walnuts, chopped
1½	cups mayonnaise
2	tablespoons finest quality curry

pinch of turmeric
salt and pepper to taste

Mix all of the ingredients and refrigerate overnight.

PORCINI MUSHROOM RISOTTO

SERVES 8

½	cup extra virgin olive oil
2	large cloves garlic, chopped
1	pound fresh porcini mushrooms or one 3 oz. package dried
¾	cup Italian parsley, chopped
2	sticks butter
1	cup chopped onion
1	pound Italian Arborio rice
6	cups chicken stock
¾	cup white wine
1	cup freshly grated Parmesan cheese

salt and pepper to taste

Saute the garlic, mushroom and parsley in olive oil. Set aside.

Saute the onion in butter and then add the rice. Cook until the rice is opaque. Add the stock, ½ cup at a time, stirring until absorbed. Keep adding stock until the rice is cooked. Add the wine. When the rice is cooked and creamy, add the mushroom mixture and sprinkle Parmesan on top. Serve hot.

Ed. Note: *We love this risotto. It is rich-tasting yet light and the flavor of the mushrooms stands out. With vegetable broth substituted for chicken stock, this would make a great vegetarian dish.*

TELLURIDE BARS

MAKES APPROXIMATELY 32 BARS

THE SHORTBREAD (BASE):

1¼	cups flour
¼	cup sugar
4	tablespoons margarine
6	tablespoons butter

Sift the flour and sugar, rub in the butter and margarine. Knead into a ball. Press into the base of a greased 12" x 18" cookie sheet. Bake at 300° for 15-20 minutes until golden.

THE FILLING:

4	tablespoons margarine
4	tablespoons butter
⅝	cup soft brown sugar
¼	cup dark corn syrup
1	can sweetened condensed milk
½	teaspoon vanilla

Put the margarine, butter, sugar, syrup and condensed milk into a pan and stir over low heat until the sugar has dissolved. Bring to a boil over medium heat and keep stirring and boiling for 7 minutes. Watch carefully to keep from scorching! Add the vanilla, stir well and pour over the shortbread. Allow to cool.

THE TOPPING:

¼	pound best quality semi-sweet or dark chocolate

Melt the chocolate over a double boiler and spread over the filling. When cold, cut into 2-inch squares.

Ed. Note: *Wonderful! As much candy as cookies, these bars would dress up a simple dessert of fresh fruit or sorbet.*

Chef: Larry Guilbeaux
100 Pennington Court
Mountain Village
728-5337

PENNINGTON'S MOUNTAIN VILLAGE INN

It is entirely possible to forget about food when you're at Pennington's Mountain Village Inn, surrounded by its 360-degree postcard views of the San Juan Mountains. Steeped in the rich greens and mauves that characterize French Country Decor, Pennington's has 12 rooms, including two honeymoon suites and a family suite, each named for one of the surrounding peaks.

When hunger pangs overpower the uncanny urge to just sit and gaze at the scenery, Pennington's offers a gourmet version of what it deems the most important meal of the day: breakfast. Chef Larry Guilbeaux, who studied at the Culinary Institute of America and completed a three-month exchange program in Europe, changes his breakfast menu daily, but always provides Inn guests and breakfast patrons with two imaginative entrees and a healthy selection of "standard fare" (eggs, juices, coffee, cereal, bacon, potatoes, Eggs Benedict, French toast, etc).

Entrees might include High Country Chicken Hash (diced chicken breast, potatoes, onions, sweet peppers and herbs topped with eggs); Huevos de San Miguel (fried corn tortilla strips served with green chiles and grated cheddar cheese tossed with scrambled eggs and served with salsa); and Very Berry Oatmeal Cakes (oatmeal pancakes smothered with sweet summer strawberries, blueberries, raspberries and blackberries).

Overlooking the 12th hole of the Telluride golf course, Pennington's is open year-round. Inn guests receive breakfast as part of their room package, while non-guests are invited to call the night before and reserve a place at breakfast.

JUDY'S SOUR CREAM BANANA BREAD

3	eggs
1	cup oil
2	cups sugar
1	tablespoon vanilla
2	cups crushed banana (4-5 medium)
1	cup sour cream
3	cups all-purpose flour
2	teaspoons baking soda
1	teaspoon salt
½	teaspoon baking powder
1	cup chopped walnuts (optional)
1	cup raisins (optional)

With a rotary mixer, beat the eggs. Add the oil, sugar and vanilla. Continue beating until thick and foamy. Add the crushed banana and sour cream and keep mixing at low speed.

In a large bowl, combine the flour, baking soda, salt and baking powder. Gently stir into the banana mixture. Add walnuts and/or raisins if desired.

Divide the batter equally between two greased, floured 5" x 9" loaf pans. Bake at 375° for 55 minutes or until a wooden pick comes out clean. Cool in the pan for 10 minutes and then turn out onto wire racks and cool thoroughly.

This bread can be frozen. Wrap it in a double layer of plastic wrap and it's fine in the freezer for several months. When thawed and warmed in the oven or microwave, it tastes as good as the day it was baked.

Enjoy!!

High Altitude Recipe: Refer to page 12

TOASTED ALMOND-APRICOT PANCAKES

SERVES 4

APRICOT SAUCE:

8-10 apricots
½ cup sugar (adjust according to the fruit's sweetness)
¼ cup water
1 tablespoon butter (optional)

Peel the apricots and remove the seeds. Place the apricots in a food processor and process to the consistency of a smooth puree. Pour the puree into a heavy pan. Over medium heat, add the sugar, water and the optional butter. Bring the mixture to a low boil, stirring frequently. When it boils, lower the heat and simmer for 15 to 20 minutes.

TOASTED ALMONDS:

¾ cup sliced almonds
vegetable spray

Spray a large, heavy skillet with vegetable spray. Heat the skillet and add the almonds. Stir frequently to ensure that all the almonds are evenly toasted. Remove from heat and cool.

PANCAKES:

1 cup all-purpose flour
1½ tablespoons sugar
2 teaspoons baking powder
¼ teaspoon salt
1 egg, beaten
1 cup milk
2 tablespoons cooking oil or melted butter

In a mixing bowl, combine the flour, sugar, baking powder, salt and toasted almonds. In another bowl, combine the beaten egg, milk and oil or butter. Add the egg and milk mixture to the dry mixture all at once. Stir until just blended. Pour ⅓ cup of batter at a time onto a hot, lightly greased griddle or skillet. Cook until golden brown. Serve with hot apricot sauce.

High Altitude Recipe: Refer to page 12

Early morning rumblings above the Idorado Mine

CHEF LARRY'S BIG MAMOU BREAKFAST CRAWFISH CAKES

Mamou is a small town in Louisiana in the heart of Cajun crawfish country.

SERVES 4

1	jumbo red onion, diced
4	tablespoons butter
1	bell pepper, diced
1	pound crawfish tails
¼	oz. chopped fresh basil
3	large eggs
2	cups plain breadcrumbs
1	cup flour
1	bunch green onions, sliced

salt, black pepper and cayenne to taste

EGG WASH:
2   large eggs beaten with 1 cup of milk

Saute the onion and pepper in butter for 5 to 7 minutes. Add ¾ pound of crawfish. Cook until all the liquid has evaporated. Add the basil and cook for another 5 minutes.

Remove from heat and place in a food processor. Pulse until finely chopped, then add the eggs. Place the mixture in a large bowl and fold in 1 cup of breadcrumbs. Fold in the remaining crawfish and season with salt, black pepper and cayenne to taste.

Portion 8 equal-sized patties. Lightly flour each patty and place in the egg wash. Combine the other cup of breadcrumbs with the flour and place each crawfish cake in the crumb mixture.

Saute in oil until golden brown. Place a poached egg on top of each cake, top with hollandaise sauce and garnish with green onion.

San Sophia Bed & Breakfast

Owners: Gary & Dianne Eschman
330 West Pacific Street
728-3001

SAN SOPHIA BED & BREAKFAST

Gary and Dianne Eschman opened their quaint and comfortable San Sophia Bed & Breakfast in December 1988. Telluride residents since 1986, the Eschmans owned a softwear company in Iowa City before entering the world of Telluride lodging.

"We had visited Telluride before we moved and, like most everyone, had fallen in love with the San Juans and the town," says Dianne. "After we sold our company, we sat down and made a list of the different businesses that could succeed in Telluride."

The result of their brainstorming is the 16-room San Sophia Bed & Breakfast on Pacific Avenue. Housed in a charming Victorian, the inn is an eclectic blend of the colors of the Southwest: blue, terra-cotta and jade. Each room is individually decorated with custom fabrics and features a brass bed covered with handmade quilts.

Guests at the San Sophia never go hungry. Mornings begin with a full breakfast buffet complete with hot and cold entrees, homemade breads and muffins, a variety of fresh fruit and juices, and yogurt in several flavors. Favorite breakfast items include crepes filled with blueberries and pecans, the mushroom omelet and homemade cinnamon rolls.

While the cozy ambiance makes it the perfect place for a romantic getaway or a little R & R, the San Sophia is popular with all sorts of groups, including a team of NASA scientists with a bad sense of humor, who couldn't resist telling the Eschmans that their breakfast was "out of this world."

CANTALOUPE WITH CHOCOLATE CHIP WAFFLES

SERVES 4 TO 6

"One morning, as I was preparing both waffles and cantaloupe melon balls, some of the juice from the melon squirted into the waffle batter and...'Mercy me, Ms. Scarlett, that tastes nice!' With the addition of chocolate chips, this decadent breakfast treat was born. This breakfast delight ABSOLUTELY must be served with sweetened whipped cream."
- *Sally Wilkinson*

CANTALOUPE JUICE:

Begin by grating enough cantaloupe to yield at least one cup of juice. In a strainer, with the back of a spoon, press the grated melon to extract all the juice. This may be done the night before, covered tightly and refrigerated.

THE WAFFLES:

Use your favorite waffle recipe or mix. This recipe was tested with Krusteaz mix.

Substitute about ¾ of the liquid called for in the batter with cantaloupe juice.

Then, grate a second piece of cantaloupe (½ to ¾ cup) and add it and ½ cup of chocolate chips to the batter.

Cook according to your waffle iron's directions and top with sweetened whipped cream.

Really easy and really good!

DIANE'S TRINITY BLACK BEAN CHILI

SERVES 8-10

"This recipe is the result of 20 years of experimentation in the quest for the Perfect Chili. Portions of this mixture came from ideas given to me while talking with Mexicans, American Indians, my Mom and a cowboy in Datil, New Mexico - all chili lovers, one way or another. I think we finally got it right." - *Dianne Eschman*

2	tablespoons peanut oil
2	large onions, chopped
2	tablespoons chopped garlic
2½	pounds ground buffalo or elk (or ground beef or turkey)
¼	cup masa harina (Mexican corn flour)
1	18 oz can Italian tomatoes, chopped
1	28 oz can tomato puree
4	tablespoons chili powder
2	tablespoons ground cumin
1	teaspoon oregano
1	tablespoon cinnamon
1	teaspoon black pepper
1	tablespoon (or less) salt
2	tablespoons cider vinegar
2	tablespoons unsweetened cocoa
2	chopped chipolte peppers in adobo sauce (available in cans in the grocery's Mexican food section)
2	16 oz. cans black beans, drained and rinsed
½	bunch fresh cilantro, chopped

In a large Dutch Oven, heat the oil over moderate heat until rippling. Add the onion and saute until golden brown; about 10 minutes. Add the garlic and saute for 2 more minutes. Add the buffalo or elk and cook, stirring until the meat loses its red color.

Sprinkle the mixture with masa harina. Stir until incorporated and cooked through; about 2 minutes.

Continued on page 138

Stir in the remaining ingredients, except the black beans and cilantro. Turn heat to high and bring to a simmer. Immediately turn to low and cover, cooking for 90 minutes, stirring occasionally to keep it from sticking. Add the black beans and cilantro and cook for 10 more minutes.

Serve hot, or cool to room temperature and store in the fridge for several days. Bring back to room temperature and re-heat over medium-low heat. Garnishes: Spoon on sour cream and/or grated cheddar cheese.

SAN SOPHIA CORNBREAD

SERVES 6 TO 8

"The basis for this cornbread began 18 years ago with a recipe acquired from a tribe of Oneida Indians living on the northern coast of Lake Superior. I've continually modified it over the years, with a major breakthrough coming when I moved to the Southwest (in lots of ways). After trying this moist recipe, be prepared to never want to eat any other cornbread again." - *Dianne Eschman*

1¼	cups cornmeal
2½	cups flour
1	cup sugar
1½	teaspoons salt
3	tablespoons baking powder
½	cup powdered milk
3	eggs
2	cups whole milk
¾	cup salad oil
1	8oz. can chopped green chiles
2	cups grated cheddar cheese

Mix the dry ingredients together. In a separate bowl, mix the eggs, milk and oil and add to the dry ingredients. Add the chopped chiles and grated cheese and stir to mix.

Grease the bottom and sides of a 9" x 13" pan. Pour in the batter and bake at 325° for 35 minutes.

 High Altitude Recipe: Refer to page 12

STRAWBERRY & CHOCOLATE CHIP MUFFINS

MAKES 18 MUFFINS

"We at the San Sophia like CHOCOLATE! Breakfast should never be mundane and monotonous. Plus, you need heavy-duty carbo-loading for the average day in Telluride!"   - *Sally Wilkinson*

8	tablespoons butter or margarine
1	cup sugar
2	cups all-purpose flour
1½	teaspoons baking powder
½	teaspoon salt
2	extra large eggs
1	cup milk
¾	pint fresh or unsweetened frozen strawberries
⅓-½	cup chocolate chips (or more!)

Cream the butter and sugar together. Add the eggs one at a time (do not overbeat at high altitude).

In a separate bowl, mix the flour, baking powder and salt. Alternately mix the flour and the milk into the butter. Stir in the strawberries and chocolate chips.

Pour into (greased or muffin paper-lined) muffin tins and bake at 400° for 22 minutes or until finger pressure does not make an indentation.

Ed. Note: *Love the strawberries and chocolate together!*

 High Altitude Recipe: Refer to page 12

SWEDE-FINN HALL

Owner: David Wolf
Chef: Mike Schuyler
472 West Pacific Street
728-2085

SWEDE-FINN HALL

Stepping into the Swede-Finn Hall, located at the corner of West Pacific Avenue and Townsend Street, you are entering the scene of a great deal of history. The old social hall is named for the Swedish speaking Finns who lived in Telluride during the early mining days. The current interior, with its green trim, black wainscoting and cream-colored wall paint, has been created to resemble early Telluride. Before being turned into a restaurant and pool hall in 1991 by current owner Dave Wolf, the building served, at different times, as a community hall, a storage room, a church and a basketball court.

Built in 1899 by a fraternal organization of Swede-Finns called the Royal Order of the Runeberg, the hall was rented out to the Telluride community for a variety of events, including the town Christmas party, which packed the narrow room with seasonal revelers each year from the 1930s to the 1950s. The Swede-Finn was also the site of a good deal of Aqua Vit-induced gaiety, even in the days of prohibition, when patrons would imbibe illicit spirits on the back steps.

According to Wolf, whose striking black and white photographs of the San Juan Mountains adorn the walls, the restaurant's menu can be described as New American, with an innovative selection of vegetarian, meat and poultry dishes. Says Chef Mike Schuyler, "The food represents an eclectic blend of ingredients and influences. I try to interject Southwestern ideas into old family favorites and surprise diners with the unexpected."

Such treats include pecan crusted quail, blackened pork chops, elk enchiladas, vegetarian shepherd's pie, linguini Swede-Finn with homemade meat or tofu balls, and grilled elk chops with a fresh blackberry brandy demi-glaze. The restaurant also offers a variety of appetizers, salads, desserts and a dozen regional and global micro-brewery beers on tap, including Guinness, Newcastle Brown Ale, Fat Tire Ale and Buffalo Gold. Sorry, no Aqua Vit.

ARTICHOKE DIP

SERVES 6 TO 8

1	28 oz. can artichoke hearts, drained, rinsed and finely chopped
1	cup finely grated Romano cheese
2	serrano chile peppers, seeded and finely chopped
½	cup mayonnaise
½	teaspoon paprika
½	tablespoon Worcestershire sauce

Mix all of the ingredients and pour into an oven-proof casserole dish. Bake at 350° for 40 minutes. Serve with toasted pita bread wedges.

The rewards of basin trekking

ATHENIAN CHICKEN PASTA

SERVES 4

4	boneless, skinless chicken breasts cut into strips
½	cup extra virgin olive oil
3-4	teaspoons chopped garlic
1	cup chopped red onion
1	cup chopped tomato
1	cup chopped red bell pepper
½	teaspoon thyme
½	teaspoon basil

generous pinch of crushed red pepper
generous pinch of salt

1	cup dry white wine
6	cups fresh spinach leaves
8	tablespoons Feta cheese
4	tablespoons pine nuts
1	pound farfalle pasta

Heat the oil in a large saute pan over medium heat. Toss the chicken in flour to coat, shake off excess and saute.

When the chicken is lightly browned, add the garlic and onion. Toss for a few seconds, then add the tomato and seasonings. Reduce the heat to low and add the white wine. Swirl the pan to incorporate the ingredients.

Add the spinach and toss. Sprinkle the pine nuts and Feta over the top of the dish and continue cooking just until the spinach wilts and the Feta melts.

Serve over cooked pasta.

Ed. Note: *With the omission of the chicken this would make an excellent vegetarian dinner.*

CHOCOLATE MOUSSE CAKE

THE CRUST:

1 cup Oreo cookie crumbs
4 tablespoons butter

 Melt the butter and add it to the crumbs. Mix together and press into a cake pan.

THE FILLING:

2 cups heavy cream, whipped stiff
6 tablespoons powdered sugar
4 egg whites
16 oz. semi-sweet chocolate
4 egg yolks
2 eggs

 Whip the cream with the sugar.
In a separate bowl, whip the whites until stiff but not dry.
Melt the chocolate and beat with the yolks and whole eggs.
Fold the whipped cream and whites, ⅓ at a time, into the chocolate.
Pour into the crust. Chill for at least 4 hours before serving.

BAILEY'S CHEESECAKE

THE CRUST:

2	cups graham cracker crumbs
½	cup sugar
8	tablespoons unsalted butter, melted

Coat a spring form pan with 1 tablespoon of melted butter. Mix the graham cracker crumbs, sugar and the other 7 tablespoons of melted butter. Press into a pan and freeze.

THE FILLING:

2½	pounds cream cheese
1½	cups sugar
5	large eggs, at room temperature
1	tablespoon vanilla
1	cup Bailey's Irish Cream

Bring the eggs and cream to room temperature. Beat the cream cheese with 1½ cups of sugar until creamy. Add the eggs, one at a time until each is thoroughly mixed in. Stir in the vanilla and the Bailey's. Pour into the chilled crust and bake at 325°F for 90 minutes.

The Tavern
at the VILLAGE

Owners: Will Kennedy & Mike Courter
Chef: Tim Schrope
117 Lost Creek Lane
Mountain Village
728-0741

THE TAVERN

When The Tavern opened its rustic doors in January 1995, it immediately glowed under the wattage of star power: Emilio Estevez and Paula Abdul dined in the new Mountain Village eatery, followed soon after by singer Mariah Carey and actors Tom Cruise and Nicole Kidman. However, owner Will Kennedy will tell you that most of the time, his restaurant is filled with ordinary folks, say, the CEO of a major corporation.

Designed in the manner of the traditional New England ski lodge of the 50s and 60s, The Tavern goes all out to make patrons as comfortable and relaxed as possible. Opting not to fill every corner with tables, Kennedy and his partner, Mike Courter, dedicated ample space to seating and a large stone fireplace.

The interior is a history lesson of sorts. The beam above the fireplace came from an Indiana Studebaker buggy factory in business in the 1800s. There are also antique snow shoes, skis and a sled (Rosebud?). The grand dame of the collection is the century-old Brunswick bar. Crafted of yellow oak and mahogany, the bar arrived by a mule train at the turn of the century and has had several homes, including the old Sheridan Pool Hall in the town of Telluride.

The Tavern's menu, overseen by chef Tim Schrope, is a study in upscale American cuisine. Dinner favorites include fried squash blossoms stuffed with goat cheese; charred beef tenderloin with jicama salad and chipolte-hazelnut sauce; basil crusted salmon with roasted vegetable couscous and mint oil; and grilled quail with mission figs, smoked slab bacon and arugula. For lunch, try the grilled shrimp and panzanella salad, the salmon club sandwich or a roasted vegetable pizza. Desserts are pleasingly decadent and include chevre cheesecake with poached pears, and wild berry shortcake with fresh cream.

Kennedy, a former commodities trader from Chicago who entered the restaurant business in Vail before moving to Telluride seven years ago, is intent on keeping The Tavern informal and inviting. "The mood is relaxed and the food is substantial," he says. "This is not Nouvelle Cuisine. You can expect decent portions at The Tavern, as well as a fine dining experience."

ROAST AUTUMN SQUASH SOUP

SERVES 4

1	large butternut squash, peeled, seeded and cut into 1" cubes
½	large yellow onion, chopped
4	ribs celery
3	cloves garlic
4	cups vegetable broth
¼	teaspoon cinnamon
¼	teaspoon ground ginger
¼	teaspoon ground nutmeg
½	tablespoon salt
½	tablespoon black pepper
1	cup heavy cream

Place the squash, celery, onion, celery and garlic in a roasting pan and roast for 60 minutes at 400°.

Remove the vegetables from the pan and place them in a stock pot with the broth, seasonings and cream. Simmer for 90 minutes.

Pour the soup into a blender or food processor and puree to a smooth consistency. Garnish with fresh nutmeg and cream.

ROAST SPAGHETTI SQUASH WITH ARTICHOKE HEARTS IN A SAFFRON-TOMATO SAUCE

SERVES 2

1	large spaghetti squash
12	cloves garlic, peeled
11	oz. artichoke hearts
2	cups tomato sauce
1	small pinch saffron

fresh oregano and basil

Split the squash lengthwise and remove the seeds. Brush the insides with olive oil and season with salt and pepper. Roast cut-side down on a cookie sheet for 60 minutes at 400°. Add the garlic and roast for 20 more minutes.

In a sauce pan, place the drained artichoke hearts, garlic, tomato sauce and saffron. Simmer for 10 minutes to bring the flavors together.

When the squash is soft, remove the insides with a fork. Season the squash with salt and pepper. Serve hot with the sauce over the top.

Garnish with fresh oregano and basil.

GRILLED QUAIL WITH CIDER-CALVADOS SAUCE

SERVES 4

THE SAUCE:

1	cup chicken stock
¼	cup apple cider
cornstarch	
1	oz. Calvados

In a sauce pot, bring the chicken stock to a boil. Lower the heat and simmer until the stock is reduced by half. Add the apple cider and let simmer for 5 minutes. Thicken with cornstarch and water. Add the Calvados and remove from heat.

THE QUAIL:

8	quail
salt and pepper	

Prepare the quail by removing the tip and the first wing section. Season with salt and pepper to taste and grill for 4 minutes on each side.

Serve the quail over a mixed organic green salad and border with wild rice. Ladle 1½ oz. of sauce over the quail. Garnish with Granny Smith apple slices.

Ice capades

The Telluride Kitchen

creative catering since 1989

Owner: Salli Russell
728-4645

TELLURIDE KITCHEN

Caterer Salli Russell uses the word "outrageous" quite often when describing her culinary calling cards. "I try to celebrate the flavors of food in my cooking," she says. "I like to do so in unusual combinations of flavors that I like to describe as outrageous."

Surprise is Russell's forte, both in preparation and presentation, and Telluride Kitchen has created some interesting and unusual meals. Her chicken ravioli, for instance, is served with escargot sauteed in roasted garlic and accented with a side of caviar. Smoked duck tacos with a kiwi, mango, red onion and avocado salsa; pan fried Rocky Mountain trout with a New Orleans-inspired butter pecan and bourbon sauce; and tiger shrimp stuffed with lobster mousse and served on a bed of leek cream sauce.

Russell moved to Telluride from Los Angeles 22 years ago, seeking the tranquility of the mountains and the allure of a small town. Her initial venture was a travel agency, Telluride's first. After a variety of jobs in what she terms "Telluride's corporate world," she opened her catering business in 1989. Her credits include serving Colorado Governor Roy Romer and his Cabinet, the staff of Good Morning America and once preparing 700 dinners in a single weekend. Catering has also taken Russell to some unique places, including the top of Ophir Pass where she served an eight course, white-glove lunch to a group of corporate executives.

"My catering style is eclectic," she says. "The needs and tastes of Telluride are so varied, you have to be able to accommodate just about anything. We do high-end gourmet and we do barbecues. We can do it all."

AUSTRIAN GARLIC SOUP

"Don't be turned off by the amount of garlic in this soup; slow cooking allows the flavors to mellow and blend, creating a wonderfully smooth-textured soup with only a hint of garlic."

6	oz. bacon, finely chopped (or 2 oz. olive oil and 4 tablespoons butter)
2	pounds onions, chopped (or 4 large leeks - white parts only)
2	cups garlic cloves (about four large bulbs), peeled and chopped
2	quarts chicken stock
2	cups coarsely chopped day-old French bread
8	parsley stems
10	sprigs fresh thyme or 1½ teaspoons dried
1	bay leaf
1	teaspoon salt
¼	teaspoon white pepper
2	cups half & half
croutons	

Fry the bacon (or heat the olive oil and butter). Then, add the onion and garlic. Cook, covered, over low heat until the onion and garlic are very soft and begin to turn golden; about 30 minutes. Increase the heat to moderate, remove the cover and continue to cook until the mixture turns a deeper golden color. Stir often.

Add the chicken stock, bread crumbs, herbs, salt and pepper. Bring to a boil, then reduce the heat and simmer for 20 to 25 minutes. Remove the herbs from the stock, puree the soup in a food processor and return to the pot. Add the half & half. Reheat, check for seasoning and serve with croutons.

RAVIOLI WITH SHIITAKE MUSHROOMS

SERVES 6

1	package favorite cheese or chicken ravioli (the larger size the better)
½	cup chicken broth
1	pound Shiitake mushrooms
2-3	cloves garlic
½	cup fresh basil leaves, shredded, plus extra for garnish
¼	cup olive oil

salt and black pepper to taste

Cook the ravioli according to the package directions. Place the cooked ravioli in the chicken broth to remain moist. Cover and keep warm.

Meanwhile, clean and cut the mushrooms into strips, discarding the tough stems. Heat the olive oil and add the mushrooms, cooking until just tender.

Peel the garlic and mash it with ¼ teaspoon salt. Add to the mushrooms along with the basil.

Serve the ravioli as an appetizer on individual plates. Put a little chicken broth on each plate. Place ¼ cup of the mushroom mixture on top of the ravioli and garnish with a basil leaf on the side.

PASTA WITH GRILLED VEGETABLES & PESTO

SERVES 4 TO 6

1	pound spaghetti
1	large zucchini, sliced diagonally
1	small eggplant, peeled and sliced into 1" strips
½	pound mushrooms
1	red bell pepper, roasted, peeled and seeded
1	green bell pepper, roasted, peeled and seeded
½	cup olive oil

dash of Mirin seasoning
dash of soy sauce

½	pound Roma tomatoes, quartered
1	bulb garlic, peeled and crushed with salt
½	teaspoon crushed red pepper
1	cup chopped fresh basil

shaved Asiago cheese for topping
salt and pepper to taste

¼	cup pesto

Combine the zucchini, eggplant, mushrooms and red and green peppers (sliced into eighths) with ¼ cup olive oil, Mirin and soy sauce. Allow to marinate for 30 minutes or longer.

Meanwhile, prepare the pasta according to the package directions.

Saute the marinated vegetables al dente in the remaining olive oil. Add the tomatoes, garlic, crushed red pepper and basil and continue cooking until the flavors are blended; about 10 minutes.

Drain the pasta and toss with the pesto. Add the sauteed vegetables, top with Asiago cheese and enjoy!

P.S. *Marinated, grilled and sliced chicken may also be added after tossing the vegetables into the pasta.*

San Juans solitude

Owners: Mike Courter & Will Kennedy
333 West Colorado Avenue
728-6344

T-RIDE COUNTRY CLUB

While the name T-Ride Country Club might connote a certain sense of exclusivity, this particular downtown restaurant holds no such pretensions. Described by co-owner Mike Courter as "a casual, family style restaurant," T-Ride is a steak house on one side and a sports bar on the other, with a satellite dish that pipes in countless games to numerous large-screen televisions positioned around the bar.

The dining room menu features prime rib, filet mignon, New York strip and pepper steaks and St. Louis-style pork ribs. T-Ride also offers sauteed bay scallops, fish and chips, grilled salmon, chicken cordon bleu, seafood linguini, garden vegetable linguini and seaside chowder. The appetizer menu, which is also served in the bar, includes calientitas (batter-dipped jalapeno peppers stuffed with cream cheese), smoked trout, jumbo butterfly prawns and calamari steak.

Courter, who has a background in business, moved to Telluride from New Jersey ten years ago not knowing whether the San Juans would become his new home. After several previous business ventures in the area, he decided to open T-Ride in 1988. Now, he says, he has no intentions of ever leaving.

SEASIDE CHOWDER

SERVES 4 TO 6

⅛	pound bacon
½	yellow onion, diced
2	cups diced celery
¼-½	cup flour (depending on how thick of a chowder you like)
8	tablespoons butter
1½	teaspoons chopped garlic
2	cups diced, cooked potatoes
¾	teaspoon salt
⅓	teaspoon black pepper
1	small bay leaf
¾	teaspoon lobster base
3	cups half & half
2	cup heavy cream
3	cups clam juice
2	6½ oz. cans chopped clams with juice
⅓	pound fresh bay scallops
¼	pound cod
⅛	pound shrimp
¼	pound salmon

In a large soup pot, saute the bacon until cooked. Add the onion and celery and cook until soft. Add the butter. When it is melted, add the flour and cook for 15 minutes over medium heat. Add the garlic, salt, pepper, clams, clam juice and lobster base.

In a separate pan, saute the fresh seafoods until medium rare.

Add half & half and heavy cream to the stock pot. Warm to thicken, then add the sauteed seafood. Cook over medium heat for 15 minutes and serve.

A representative of Telluride's infamous valley cows

Owners: Hope Anderson & Joan Sullivan
Chef: Bob Scherner
221 South Oak Street
728-9507

221 SOUTH OAK

221 South Oak has an almost cult following in Telluride. I've even heard one local say you might as well leave town during off-season because 221 closes then. The burgeoning popularity of this cozy bistro has as much to do with its atmosphere as its acclaimed cuisine: serenity basks the dining room like alpenglow and there's a sense of hushed but thorough enjoyment and elegance throughout.

Owners Hope Anderson and Joan Sullivan opened 221 in December 1992, choosing for their location a historic home nestled among the stately trees of south Oak Street. When it came time to christen the restaurant, giving it a name identical to its address seemed both logical and unique.

The owners' goal was to create an atmosphere that would induce an almost hypnotic sense of relaxation and comfort. Rather than fill the entire space with tables, Anderson and Sullivan placed inviting, earth-toned couches and a large woodburning stove in the center of the front room. They adorned the walls with gold-framed oil paintings, added subtle lighting and surrounded this mini living room with 11 elegant tables.

They then found a chef whose artistry could match the physical surroundings: Bob Scherner. Scherner, an expert mogul skier, attended the Western Culinary Institute in Portland, Oregon and worked in Boulder and Chicago restaurants before coming to Telluride. He describes his food as "eclectic, clean and simple."

Favorites include seared tuna with warm spinach salad, served with shrimp dumplings in a citrus soy vinaigrette; smoked salmon with pickled baby beets and a mustard vinaigrette; and a goat cheese strudel wrapped in filo and served with a citrus vinaigrette and diced Asian pears.

Textures and flavors are important to Scherner and his creations celebrate the diversity of the ingredients. "We always strive for a course with contrasting elements, so none of the individual ingredients is lost." The above-mentioned goat cheese strudel, for instance, combines the creaminess of the cheese with the crunchiness of the filo, and sets off the sweetness of the pears with the tartness of the cheese. "Our goal is to retain the integrity of the foods from the beginning of the meal to the end."

SALAD OF GRILLED TELLURIDE BOLETES WITH TAT SOI, TEARDROP TOMATOES, ROMANO & A ROSEMARY VINAIGRETTE

SERVES 6

ROSEMARY VINAIGRETTE:

1	cup veal stock
2	tablespoons red wine vinegar (more or less to taste)
5	cloves roasted garlic
¼	cup extra virgin olive oil
salt and pepper	
2	sprigs fresh rosemary

Combine the stock, vinegar, garlic and olive oil in a sauce pan and bring to a boil. Remove and puree in a blender (Be careful!). Remove and strain. Season to taste with salt and pepper and keep warm.

[Note: *Veal stock goes very well with the richness of the mushrooms and makes the dish more red-wine friendly. If veal stock is unavailable, omit and add more olive oil and vinegar.*]

THE SALAD:

3	pounds Bolete mushrooms (also called Cepes or Porcinis), cleaned with a brush and cut into ½" strips
½	pound Tat Soi (small Japanese cabbage leaf)
1	pint teardrop tomatoes
½	cup grated Pecorino Romano
olive oil	
salt and pepper	

Brush the Boletes with olive oil, salt and pepper. Grill for 1-2 minutes and place over the Tat Soi. Sprinkle the tomatoes around and the cheese on top. Give the plate a quick "flash" in the oven (400°) and dress with vinaigrette.

POLENTA CRUSTED SOFT SHELL CRAB, ROASTED SUNBURST SQUASH & GOLD PEPPER BROTH

SERVES 6

6   jumbo soft shell crabs from Chesapeake Bay, cleaned
½   cup unbleached white flour
½   cup polenta or coarse cornmeal
10-12 baby sunburst squash, quartered
2-3   shallots
2-3   cloves garlic
2-3   large gold peppers, roasted, peeled, seeded and chopped
1   cup fish fume (stock)
salt and pepper
olive oil and butter

THE SAUCE:

Cook the garlic and shallots gently in olive oil until translucent. Add the chopped peppers and fish fume and bring to a boil. Puree in a blender and strain. Season with salt and pepper and keep hot.

THE CRABS:

Mix the flour and cornmeal together with salt and pepper. Clean the crabs by removing face and gills with scissors. Also, cut pointed "wings" on both ends (this will prevent the crabs from popping).

Heat a saute pan over high heat. Add olive oil and floured crabs. Add one tablespoon butter per two crabs and let crabs brown. Flip and finish in a 400° oven for 3-4 minutes.

In the meantime, toss the squash with olive oil, salt and pepper and roast in the oven on a baking sheet until lightly browned; 3-4 minutes.

Present the dish by cutting the crabs in half and standing them up in the middle of a pasta bowl with the squash in the center. Pour a generous amount of sauce over each crab. Garnish with chopped fresh basil.

Trout Lake

GRILLED GULF SWORDFISH WITH HERB BASMATI RICE, ROASTED CUSTALANO TOMATO, OLIVES, PINE NUTS & SAFFRON BROTH

SERVES 6

6	6 oz. swordfish steaks
	herb mix to include: parsley, basil, dill, tarragon and chives, equaling ¼ cup
2	cups brown basmati rice
4	cups water
salt and pepper to taste	
6	custalano or heirloom tomatoes, cut into thirds
½	cup mild olives such as Nicoise or Amphisa, pitted and chopped
½	cup toasted pine nuts
2	cups fish fume
1	tablespoon saffron

Heat the fume to a boil and bloom the saffron. Simmer for 3-4 minutes and strain.

Cook the rice in water until tender. Toss with herbs.

Brush the tomatoes with olive oil, salt and pepper and roast at 450° for 2-3 minutes.

Season and grill the swordfish steaks for 2-3 minutes on each side until medium.

In a large pasta bowl, place the rice in the center with olives and pine nuts around. Place 3 tomato thirds around and swordfish on top of the rice. Season to taste.

Pour the saffron fume over the swordfish and serve.

OREGON LAMB LOIN, CANNELLINI BEAN RAGOUT & SAGE REDUCTION

SERVES 6

3	pounds Oregon lamb loin, trimmed (approximately 6 chops)
½	pound cannellini beans
½	pound organic onion, cut into large chunks
½	pound organic carrots, cut into large chunks
½	pound organic celery, cut into large chunks
½	pound French beans
¼	cup roasted garlic, whole
3	cups lamb stock
2	tablespoons fresh sage, chopped

Cook the beans in salted water with the onion, carrot and celery for about an hour or more, until the beans are tender. Drain, cool and discard the vegetables.

Blanch the French beans until tender, cool in an ice water bath.

Brush the garlic with a small amount of olive oil and roast at 300° for 30-45 minutes, until mild and tender.

Season the lamb with salt and pepper and grill or saute to medium rare; about 2 minutes per side.

Place the cannellini beans, French beans, garlic and sage in a sauce pot and add lamb stock to cover. Heat and season with salt and pepper.

Serve by placing ½ cup of ragout on each plate. Slice the lamb at a bias and fan across the ragout. Drizzle more sauce if desired.

Ed. Note: *The cannellini bean ragout is so good that it could be made with vegetable broth and eaten on its own, or with rice and/or French bread. This recipe could work equally well with a leg of lamb, roasted rare.*

The Columbine - Colorado's state flower

WARM COLORADO PEACH TART WITH BLACK RASPBERRIES, VANILLA, MASCARPONE ICE CREAM & CARAMEL SAUCE

SERVES 4 TO 6

PREPARE PEACHES:

Peel, pit and dice 4 peaches. Scrape the seeds from ½ of a whole vanilla bean into the peaches and toss. Refrigerate.

THE TART SHELLS:

3	tablespoons cold butter, cut into cubes
1	cup flour
1	teaspoon poppy seeds
⅛	cup plus 2 teaspoons sugar
salt, a dash	
1	egg, slightly beaten

Place the first five ingredients in a mixer equipped with a paddle. Mix on low speed until the butter is broken into bits and worked into the dry ingredients. Add the egg and continue mixing just until the dough comes together.

Wrap the dough in plastic wrap and chill for at least one hour before use. Extra dough can be frozen.

Roll out the dough on a floured surface to a thickness of ⅛ inch. Cut out rounds and fit into tart molds. Chill for 15 minutes then bake, weighted, at 375° for 30 minutes or until golden.

THE MASCARPONE ICE CREAM:

2   egg yolks
2   tablespoons sugar
1   cup milk
3   oz. Mascarpone cheese
a dash of salt

Whisk the yolks and sugar until smooth, and the color of the yolks lightens. Bring the milk to a boil over medium heat, then pour into the yolks, whisking constantly. Return the mixture to the saucepan and whisk in the Mascarpone. Cook over medium heat, stirring constantly until it thickens enough to coat a spatula. DO NOT BOIL. Pass through a fine chinois or two layers of cheesecloth. Chill in the freezer for 15 minutes and then churn in an ice cream machine.

THE CARAMEL SAUCE:

½   cup heavy cream
4   tablespoons unsalted butter
⅛   cup light corn syrup
1   cup sugar
⅓   cup heavy cream

Place ½ cup of heavy cream and the butter in a small pot and bring to a boil. Meanwhile, combine the corn syrup and sugar in a fairly large pot and melt the sugar while stirring constantly with a wooden spoon. When the sugar turns a smooth, light straw color, remove from heat. Ladle in the already boiled cream and butter, always stirring. Return to heat and boil for 2 minutes, still stirring. Add the ⅓ cup of heavy cream and boil for 1 more minute.

ASSEMBLE THE DESSERT:

Have each baked tart shell ready. Quickly heat the prepared peaches with some blackberries in a pan. Generously fill each tart shell with warm fruit. Top with a scoop of Mascarpone ice cream and a drizzle of caramel sauce.

Ed. Note: *This is a lovely dessert which would also be good with blueberries or raspberries in summer or sauteed apples or pears in fall. The caramel sauce is especially nice and could always be drizzled over ice cream for a simple but elegant dessert.*

INDEX BY COURSE

BAKED THINGS & BREAKFAST

FISH & SEAFOOD

MEAT AND POULTRY

PASTAS

VEGETARIAN

SIDES

DESSERTS

Mountain biking on Wilson Mesa

NOTES...

NOTES...

NOTES...

NOTES...

NOTES...

NOTES...

Y'all come back now...

I0500972